Bond and Covenant

Bond and Covenant

A Perspective on Holy Matrimony
from the Book of Common Prayer

R. David Cox

 CHURCH

Church Publishing Incorporated, New York

Library of Congress Cataloging-in-Publication Data

Cox, R. David

Bond & covenant : a perspective on holy matrimony from the Book of Common Prayer /
   R. David Cox.
   p. cm.
   Includes bibliographical references
   ISBN 978-0-89869-327-0
    1. Episcopal Church. Celebration and blessing of a marriage. 2. Marriage--Religious
aspects--Episcopal Church. I. Title: Bond and covenant. II. Title.

BX5944.M3 C68 1999
264'.0355--dc21

                                      99-053176

Church Publishing Incorporated
445 Fifth Avenue
New York, NY 10016

5   4   3   2   1

*In thanksgiving for those whose marriages I have solemnized,
and for the one who teaches me most of marriage,
Melissa*

Table of Contents

Acknowledgments

*A*ny wedding involves a cast of tens, if not hundreds. So does a book about marriage. I am grateful:

- to the 300-or-so couples who invited me into the most significant event of their lives together and who, in our discussions, taught me much of the meaning of matrimony;
- to Mr. and Mrs. Robert Lundquist and to my late father for the hospitality of a place to write;
- to R. E. Lee Memorial Church in Lexington, Virginia, for the time to write and, more, for the opportunity to do what I love with people I cherish and get paid for it besides;
- to Frank Tedeschi and Church Publishing Incorporated for undertaking this book, and to Johnny Ross, my editor;
- to the Rev. Henry H. Edens, IV, the Rev. Mark A. Lattime, the Rev. Jane Sigloh, and Mr. Ralph Wiegandt for adding insights into particular issues;
- to the staff of the Leyburn Library at Washington and Lee University for opening to me its tremendous resources;
- to Andrew, Trevor, and Meredith for daily reminding me of the purpose, meaning, value, and fun of being a family;

and, above all, to Melissa who exemplifies the nature of love.

For these and so many more, thanks be to God.

Prelude

The time arrives. All the preparations, whether over the past two years or just six frantic weeks, come down to this moment. Guests assemble in the church or, perhaps, the home or park or field by water's edge. Ushers escort the mothers to their places as a latecomer straggles along, embarrassed for having misplaced the directions to the ceremony. Specially-chosen music swells from organ or string quartet or guitar; or, instead of music, the most joyous of silences.

As the groom appears with the clergy, the friends he chose as groomsmen process in, then the bridal attendants. Then she appears, radiant and beautiful, dressed with the utmost of consideration, walking slowly, purposefully, toward the equally nervous man she will marry.

The wedding has begun!

More than that, a life has begun, a new life marked by commitment and the faith and hope and love that the oft-read passage of scripture cites, and not a little of God's grace. The commitment is as profound as two people can make, for it is a commitment, a bond, and a relationship—a covenant—for life. Faith is the only way to begin that commitment, along with hope, which goes well beyond mere optimism, and a love which both transcends and undergirds romance because this love arises not just from the two of them but from God. So the couple come consciously, willingly before the Almighty, by their act seeking more than what a justice of the peace can give. They ask God's blessing, and the Church joins in prayer knowing that what they undertake is an adventure into the kingdom of God. For this is a journey in which they and those around them can discover anew the reality of the risen life of Jesus Christ, and find it—of all places—within this new creation forged in the bond these two people undertake before God.

That is what this book is about—an adventure in faith in Jesus. His resurrection brings about a new creation. Matrimony is one means of living it out, such that husband and wife can share this new life between themselves and with those around them. It is not a "how to" guide to getting married such as Amy Vanderbilt or Martha Stewart might provide; nor is it a counselor's directions on deepening the marriage relationship. Rather, it takes the ceremony of the Episcopal Church, which has been adapted by many other denominations, as a way of meditating on what Holy Matrimony means for a couple committed to abiding in their love for each other while also discovering, showing forth, and extending that love of God which is both for themselves and for the world.

For those considering marriage, this book may prompt some thought about what you are about to undertake. For those who are already married, perhaps this may inspire some reflection on the past, present, and future of your "holy estate of matrimony."

God does not call everyone to wedlock. Marrying is a vocation for some but not for all. Christians live out the risen life in varying ways. This is for those who believe that God has invited them to share his love in this vibrant way with another person, through Holy Matrimony.

Preparation

No wedding occurs without preparation, as anyone anticipating it soon discovers. Few realize how much preparation a wedding takes. More importantly, no marriage occurs without preparation any more than a house can be built without a good foundation. Getting married takes time and consideration, not only for the wedding but even more for the marriage.

In fact, building the foundation has already begun. Any wedding culminates a relationship between two people which, whether of long or short duration, never springs from nothing. In earlier cultures, the marriage may have been concocted by the parents; treaties and dowries were carefully negotiated with the innocent son or daughter as unwitting pawn at the center of the pact. Sometimes the commitment was resolved over a shotgun. Nowadays, in our culture, the man and woman arrive at their conclusion almost invariably on their own—their own schedules (usually!) and their own reasons. All of this they bring to the altar.

They also bring their own willingness to be married. No one can commit authentically to what one does not wish to do. Especially *this* commitment. For this is a lifelong dedication. Nothing less will do. Even King Canute, who, according to legend, thought himself so mighty as to command the tide to keep away, ordered that in Anglo-Saxon England "no woman or maiden shall ever be forced to marry a man whom she dislike."[1] It is not recorded whether fathers obeyed him any more than waters.

Consent forms one essential ingredient of marriage. But consent must be informed. Those entering matrimony should understand the nature of what it is to which they will pledge themselves.

Nor does marriage exist in isolation. It involves the couple's families and friends who have been intimately involved in their growing up, who may even have introduced groom to bride. It involves society, which benefits when marriages prosper and suffers when marriages fail.[2] It also involves the Church. The "community of faith" may have nurtured one or both of the couple; and to this community the couple come to be married.

The first portion of the service covers these fundamental points. An opening "Exhortation" explains the nature and importance of

Holy Matrimony. What is traditionally termed the "Betrothal" establishes that these two people *can* be married, and that they *wish* to marry each other. The service then asks the support of all the Church, for Holy Matrimony always occurs within the context of the "community of faith", the people of God who are called upon to witness the marriage, no matter where it occurs or how large or small the crowd, and to support it with its prayers and actions.

But preparations began long before the service. Early in their engagement, the couple probably approached a priest* who as- certained with them whether they could be married at all. As the preface to the service forthrightly states, "In the Episcopal Church it is required that one, at least, of the parties must be a baptized Christian; that the ceremony be attested by at least two witnesses; and that the marriage conform to the laws of the State and the canons of this Church" (BCP 422).

These requirements have two implications. For one, the clergy must make certain that the laws of the state are met. Marriage being a matter of communal concern for the wider society, the clergy act in marriage as civic agents who are commissioned for this purpose. At the same time, they remain delegates of the Church, functioning on behalf of the "community of faith" in which Holy Matrimony occurs.[3] Witnesses, too, represent the communal concern of the people of God. This practice is age-old. In ancient Israel, a marriage took place in the presence of at least ten witnesses who constituted the "minyan," the minimum necessary for a synagogue service.[4] We retain this emphasis in requiring that at least two witnesses be

---

The Book of Common Prayer (or BCP) states, "A priest or a bishop normally presides at the Celebration and Blessing of a Marriage, because such ministers alone have the function of pronouncing the nuptial blessing, and of cRelebrating the Holy Eucharist" (BCP 422). A deacon may always participate and, if civil law allows, officiate, though without giving the nuptial blessing or celebrating the Eucharist.

Usually, the rector, priest-in-charge, or assisting priest of the parish in which the couple wish to be married leads them through the preparation process and eventually presides at the marriage ceremony as "celebrant" or "officiant." Other clergy may participate or even preside, though this is the decision of the rector or priest-in-charge, through whom any such arrangement must be made.

For sake of simplicity: 1) I will refer to the celebrant or officiant as a priest, though a bishop or deacon also may so serve; 2) I may refer to the priest, celebrant, or officiant as "he," though women function in all these capacities as well.

present. The requirement that one if not both parties will have been baptized also reflects the fact that this marriage does occur within the community of faith into which one or both have been sacramentally initiated.

In the past, "banns of Marriage" helped assure that all was public and legal. On three successive weeks preceding the service, the priest or clerk of the parish would "publish" the banns—the term derives from an Anglo-Saxon word meaning "to summon" or "proclaim."[5] He would announce in church that these two people were going to wed and, "if any of you know just cause why they not be joined together in Holy Matrimony, you are bidden to declare it." Any objector had four chances—the three times when the banns were published, plus one last moment in the marriage service itself. As a result, the community was aware of the planned union; and if someone knew, for example, that the couple had a family kinship that might be considered too close, or that one had pledged himself/herself to another, or indeed was married to another, then he could object.

The banns once served to preclude clandestine marriages which for over a thousand years had created problems.[6] Need eventually faded to benign customs. In a nineteenth-century Nottinghamshire parish, when banns declared a forthcoming marriage, someone would rise and say, "God speed them well," to which the congregation responded, "Amen." Elsewhere, for a couple to have banns published and then back out was called "mocking the Church" and deemed a slight upon the community.[7] Nowadays, the banns may be little more than a quaint means of informing the Church about what will take place, and the Prayer Book provides for it (BCP 437). At heart, though, the idea of the banns reflects three aspects of the importance of matrimony: that marriage requires preparation and, therefore, time to prepare; that it is public and, thus, of social concern; and that the Christian community takes a special, corporate interest.

The civic function of the banns has been assumed by the marriage license required by local governments. Most, if not all, states have laws governing marriage. Some jurisdictions require blood tests as an indication of health and also birth certificates or other proofs of identity. Some have waiting periods to allow, as I found in a parish near a Navy base, for each to sober up before joining forever to that person who looked so enticing at that wild barroom party the night before. Other states place expiration dates on the licenses they issue. Some require the wedding to occur within the township where the license is issued, a point one couple overlooked when planning a fancy church wedding in a town adjoining the one in which they got their license. An hour before the scheduled time for the ceremony, the officiant trucked the couple and two witnesses across the city line to a parking lot where they exchanged vows, were pronounced husband and wife, signed the papers, then appeared before a congregation which had no idea that they had already been wed. The moral of that story: find out what is required by the state where you plan to be married. This is your responsibility. No license, no wedding!

Every Church, too, has some basic requirements which vary from denomination to denomination. For the Episcopal Church, canons, or laws, govern what it does.[8] Additionally, an individual parish may have particular criteria for those who wish to be married in its church, often arising out of practical experience or pragmatic necessity, if not from theological position. Mindful of the rules of church and state, as well as of the specific place, the priest generally asks such questions as the following:

1. Are you who you say you are?

This parallels the state's concern for proper identity. It is basic information—so much so that biblical tradition understood the name to reveal someone's true nature (hence the renaming of Jacob in Genesis 32:27–28 or the burning-bush discussion with Moses over God's name in Exodus 3:13–15).

2. Are you of age?

As entering into marriage is, among other things, a legal matter, both parties must be old enough to engage in a legal marital contract. Beneath that, for state and even more for Church, is the question of sufficient maturity. Age is one, though not the only, sign.

3. Are you related in any way?

For centuries, even millennia, societies have discouraged or even forbidden marriage between men and women with close blood kinship.[9] One reason for "publishing the banns" was to jog the communal memory in order to preclude some nearly-forgotten half-brother from unwittingly entering into an incestuous marriage. There were, and are, two concerns. The first is the higher incidence of genetically-related health problems among offspring of couples who are too closely related. The second is the interpersonal complexities that arise when one's in-laws are also one's own family! So while the Church does not post a flat-out prohibition (Franklin and Eleanor Roosevelt, for example, were distant cousins), the issue still is considered vitally important—one that must be recognized and examined.

4. Are you of sound mind?
Are both parties capable of knowing what they are doing?

5. Do you enter this of your own free will?
No shotgun weddings! For marriage to work, each must be willing to enter into it at the outset.

Consider the story of poor Robert fitz Geoffrey, a medieval "husband" who agreed to marry Isabel only after a violent struggle (during which he lost his nose). A court determined he had not given free consent, however, and, thus, annulled the marriage. Alas, the victory availed him little, for he had already died.[10]

The modern Episcopal Church agrees with the medieval court: free will matters![11]

6. Is at least one of you baptized?
Holy Matrimony occurs within the community of faith, which considers Holy Baptism as its sacramental entrance. It is one sign— in this case a basic one—of participation in the life of the Church such that the holiness of matrimony would be meaningful. Along that same line:

7. Are you willing to enter into Holy Matrimony within the "community of faith"?
Will you strive to abide by the holiness of matrimony as (in this case) the Episcopal Church understands it?[12] You will be asked in time to sign a statement to this effect.[13]

8. Are you or have you ever been married before?

Charlotte Brontë may have provided the most famous literary example of this impediment in *Jane Eyre*, when someone objects and Mr. Rochester admits, "There will be no wedding to-day." He had a wife, still living; and even her insanity gave no excuse for bigamy.[14]

Some years ago, newspapers ran stories of a man who had 53 wives. He would travel through the west from town to town seducing one lady after another into quickie nuptials, then head into the sunset for his next conquest. But the newspapers were wrong: he had one wife, and 52 bigamous relationships.

Having been married, whether it ended in death or divorce, is such a part of a person's past that it must be explored carefully in the pastoral discussions with a priest. (If the marriage concluded in divorce, other considerations arise, as will be noted.)

9. Do you intend for this marriage to be lifelong?

A soap-opera character who marries twelve times on television is not truly married: there is no intention of marrying "for real." True intent makes the difference. And the intent is for life. Marriage is a total commitment. Less than lifetime means less than one hundred per cent. It's as simple as that.

These questions establish a couple's ability to be married within the Church and serve a pragmatic purpose on various levels, pastoral and legal. Unless the basic conditions are right, there can be no genuine marriage as we understand it. For instance, if George promises to love, honor, and cherish Mary and vice-versa—when their real names are Melvin and Hermione—then, in fact, two strangers promise what neither can commit. Their relationship is based upon a fundamental untruth.

Or, if one or both are below the age to enter into the legal contract which is part of marriage, parents or guardians must give consent.

Clearly, too, a one hundred per cent commitment is a lifelong commitment, and without that commitment there can be no true marriage. A mini-fad of the seventies illustrates the problem. Some decided to enter into "contract marriages." Under this system, a couple would agree to love, honor, and cherish each other in total commitment for all of the next five years (or whatever the stated time was), and then review the situation. The problem, though, was perfectly obvious: They may have a bond but lack a covenant. So, midway through year three after a ferocious fight, one concludes, "I have only eighteen months left on this sentence," and there goes the incentive to make up with the other. Knowing that one is in it for life, by contrast, makes a person far more likely to resolve things with the spouse and to move forward—stronger, in fact, for what at first seemed to be so negative. Such is the nature of commitment and love.

Unfortunately, even with the best of intentions, many a marriage does not last for life. But without even the intention, it has no chance.

In light of what we believe about Holy Matrimony, divorce poses not only an excruciating personal dilemma but a major theological one as well. On the one hand, the Episcopal Church upholds the sanctity of marriage and the permanence of vows. On the other, it recognizes that, in this frail and fallen world, not all can or do live up to the vows they make, even though they made them with full intent and good conscience. Moreover, insisting on remaining in pseudo-marriages, in which the capability of attaining anything approximating those ideals has died, benefits neither the Church nor anyone else.

As a result, we recognize divorce, while exhorting those in a troubled marriage to seek assistance so that divorce becomes the very last and least desirable option. Indeed, seeking help is a canonical responsibility assumed by those who marry within the Church. Its clergy are charged with helping couples find reconciliation.[15] Endangered couples should always see a priest or other counselor in an attempt to work out their problems before engaging a lawyer.

But as some marriages do fail despite the best of efforts, the Church also provides means whereby a divorced person may marry again within the context of Holy Matrimony. The bishop of the diocese must give permission, and probably has particular rules, concerns, and processes to follow—all of which are motivated by a consideration for the well-being of everyone involved: the previous marriage, the proposed marriage, the families (especially children), and the wider community of faith.

These issues, then, establish two people's ability to be married. Any one of these could be an "impediment," to use the formal term; it impedes the ability of the couple to live out their life in Holy

Matrimony and to reach the ideals which we hold forth. I recall a husband who promised at the altar to be faithful to one woman, while another was on his mind. Within weeks he found his way into this other woman's bed. His was no marriage, doomed from the start.

In Roman Catholic circles, this would be grounds for "annulment": no true marriage ever existed. Churches have devised means of dealing with impediments: they resolve them (for example, with parental permission for the underage or with the completion of a remarriage process for divorced persons); or they recognize the impediment as just that and turn down the couple. These are rare situations, but they involve real issues at the basis of a relationship. Meeting these criteria establishes the very possibility that a couple can attain to the ideals which marriage holds. When it comes to marriage, those ideals are what we all seek—the family, the priest, the wider Christian community, above all the bride and groom.

Indeed, a concern for the well-being of all is what underlies the entire process of getting married. The Church wants for two people to discover and savor the joys which marriage holds. If it seems that procedures make getting married more difficult than, say, heading for a justice of the peace or a wedding chapel, it is because the Church takes marriage seriously and believes the nuptial vows deserve time for contemplation.

Marriage licenses, banns, questions about potential "impediments": these practical necessities focus on the legal and the "negative." They are important enough for the liturgy itself to mention, but they are also usually quickly resolved. Far more important are the "positives" of why the couple wish to get married, and why they choose *Holy* Matrimony. That's when the conversation between priest and couple gets really interesting—and exciting!

Lady Bracknell, a character in Oscar Wilde's comic play *The Importance of Being Earnest,* declared to two lovebirds, "To speak frankly, I am not in favour of long engagements. They give people the opportunity of finding out each other's character before marriage, which I think is never advisable."[16] The Church has found the opposite to be true (at least the part about finding out about each other's character). In fact, thinking about the nature of Holy

Matrimony and the couple's relationship within it—and, in the process, about each other—is another requirement of the Church.[17] It, too, is an obligation, though one of tremendous opportunity. It takes time, though couples I meet with often report that their time was well spent. As some states demand a waiting period, so certainly do churches: thirty days minimum in the Episcopal Church, although "this requirement may be dispensed with" for very good reason, with the matter reported to the bishop.[18]

This period of time allows the couple to meet with a priest or other responsible person for "premarital counseling," which becomes an opportunity for sharing backgrounds and ideas and ideals, for learning about the nature of marriage from a Christian view, and for growing together in the love not only of each other but also of Christ. Sometimes the topic is not only preparing for marriage but surviving the wedding—with important links between the two. The wedding is a day, the marriage a lifetime. Yet arranging for weddings often arouses hosts of issues worth exploring: family dynamics in general, in-laws in particular; religious practices and convictions; cultural tastes; personal quirks, old traditions or unique ideas; money; priorities; even dietary differences. For an objective, experienced third party to help negotiate the premarital predicaments can become a supportive advantage.

Because this is an intimately pastoral relationship, every priest has his or her own approach, which even may vary from couple to couple. Styles, requirements, subject matter, even the number of meetings all depend upon the priest. It is always best to contact the clergy as early as possible. The additional time facilitates not only the making of arrangements, but, even more importantly, the development of a good, relaxed relationship between the couple and the priest. Engagement is not so much a state of being as a journey into marriage. Having the priest as a companion on the journey can become tremendously helpful in making the venture even more valuable; and the ceremony becomes ever more meaningful for having as officiant one whom together you have come to know rather well.

Along the way, the couple will sign a "Declaration of Intent." This is a statement of what the Church holds as central about marriage. Just as anyone ordained in the Episcopal Church affixes his or her name to a fundamental statement of conviction, so, we ask and require all couples to do likewise, in words which anticipate the service itself:

> We, A.B. and C.D., desiring to receive the blessing of Holy Matrimony in the Church, do solemnly declare that we hold marriage to be a lifelong union of husband and wife as it is set forth in the Book of Common Prayer.
>
> We believe that the union of husband and wife, in heart, body, and mind, is intended by God for their mutual joy; for the help and comfort given one another in prosperity and adversity; and, when it is God's will, for the procreation of children and their nurture in the knowledge and love of the Lord.
>
> And we do engage ourselves, so far as in us lies, to make our utmost effort to establish this relationship and to seek God's help thereto.[19]

What, then, does the Book of Common Prayer set forth? Exploring that is part of what the premarital meetings are all about, and is the very reason for this book.

Exhortation

On the appointed day, the couple appear before the priest. At least two witnesses join them[20]; this is a public and communal occasion, as the service never lets us forget. The witnesses attest to what happens and represent the wider people of God. All then turn to the officiant, who opens the Book of Common Prayer to page 423 and begins:

> Dearly beloved: We have come together in the presence of God to witness and bless the joining together of this man and this woman in Holy Matrimony. The bond and covenant of marriage was established by God in creation, and our Lord Jesus Christ adorned this manner of life by his presence and first miracle at a wedding in Cana of Galilee. It signifies to us the mystery of the union between Christ and his Church, and Holy Scripture commends it to be honored among all people. The union of husband and wife in heart, body, and mind is intended by God for their mutual joy; for the help and comfort given one another in prosperity and adversity; and, when it is God's will, for the procreation of children and their nurture in the knowledge and love of the Lord. Therefore marriage is not to be entered into unadvisedly or lightly, but reverently, deliberately, and in accordance with the purposes for which it was instituted by God.

These are phrases and sentences packed full of meaning, far more than anyone can digest while standing before the priest. Yet they go to the heart of matrimony. Let's examine them:

We have come together in the presence of God...

We mortals hold some truths so deeply that they go without saying—but need to be said anyway. Here is one. Are we not always in the presence of God? Whether in church or in a field or at a seashore, whether skydiving or studying in the library or dining at home or taking a shower (perhaps a shocking thought), God is there. So the issue is not *where* on this earth the ceremony takes place, for God will be there, and we will stand before him.* (Some clergy will

---

*God is always greater than the English language (and its gender-specific pronouns) can convey; but—for sake of linguistic ease, and with that disclaimer—I will occasionally use a masculine pronoun to refer to God.

agree to do weddings outside of the church building and some will not[21]; that too is a matter to discuss at the outset.)

Why bother, then, to announce that we are in the presence of the One before whom we always abide? Frankly, we need the reminder to bring to consciousness a reality which Christians assume but, when reminded, we then confirm. The recollection causes us to pay new attention and sometimes to act differently, even to shape up as we know we ought. Realizing anew that God is present may affect how we think, what we say, and what we do.

On many levels we rely on those reminders to refresh what we so often take for granted. For instance, do you say "I love you" to those you truly care about—to the one you will marry or already have, or to children or parents? Most couples heading toward the altar assure me that they do. "All the time," say some.

But do they *have* to? Must you speak those words in order for there to be love?

Surely not, for then the relationship would depend upon words, as if love relied solely on what we say.

How, though, does it feel to speak those words? Probably pretty good. How does it feel to hear those words? No doubt even better. Reassured. Evokes warm and fuzzy feelings. The milk of human kindness courses afresh through the veins, all because of some words that you don't *have* to say, but which are so *good* to say and hear that you really *should* say them. They bring to awareness what you know is the case, but always deserves restating.

Take another situation. Have you ever found some evening that the one you love has had "one of those days"? So palpable is this mood "most foul" that words seem unnecessary. Initially, words are needed much less than a warm hug. But soon words *are* needed, to find out what the problem is and, if not to resolve it, at least to share it. In talking about it, the wretchedness seems to ease: You deal with it together.

In each of these examples, something you know and even take for granted is brought to the surface, articulated, and dealt with either by putting the issue to rest or by celebrating an inner reality made new and fresh by simply reaffirming what you know to be the obvious case.

Through its liturgies, the Church takes the deepest truths and expresses them in word, act, movement, song; and in that process they ideally become all the more real. We repeat the Creed and articulate belief. We pour water on someone's forehead, convinced that God's love will be poured out for that person. We offer bread and wine, vocally asking God to make them become for us the Body and Blood of Jesus. Inner realities are expressed and confirmed, made real and strengthened as things begin to happen.

Likewise, much of what the marriage service does is to raise to the surface what we know profoundly to be true. Two people will pledge their love for each other. Yes, of course; why else would they stand before the matrimonial altar? But on this occasion, in the presence of God, in front of that congregation large or small, they declare their love. They join hands, give a ring or two, and receive a blessing. As a result, they emerge qualitatively different from when they came in. The two become one, in the presence and in the eyes of God and the world.

...to witness and bless the joining together of this man and this woman in Holy Matrimony.

If it hardly needs mentioning that we are always in the presence of God, so, too, everyone present knows why they gather. Hadn't each received an invitation? If tourists arrive at the church door, won't they deduce what this woman in white is doing with that man in a tuxedo?* This announcement is another of those statements that reminds us of what we're doing, heightens our attention, raises our awareness, and thereby contributes to the excitement of what we share—which is "to witness and bless the joining together" of this couple.

Three elements here: first, the congregation "witnesses." That simple word has several important meanings.

- It holds a legal sense. Witnesses ensure on behalf of the community that all is well. Recently I signed a document which

---

Note that, according to the Prayer Book, anyone can attend: "Christian marriage is a... public covenant" (BCP 422), open to anyone who happens by. (Of course, you are not obligated—by the Prayer Book or any other authority—to invite wandering tourists to the reception afterwards!)

required another person to attest that I actually signed it; she then affixed her signature to verify what I had done. The congregation by its presence attests that these two people are getting married and that all is well in form and legalities. Everyone present thereby protects the interests of society and of the couple, because the congregation and especially the two formally designated witnesses can swear that these two individuals were duly, legally united.

- It holds a social sense. The congregation bears witness that, though intimately personal, matrimony is never private. Others are very much part of this marriage, even as this marriage concerns us all (as the prayers to be examined later in this book will show).

- Finally, the word "witness" holds a special meaning within the Church. To "witness," of course, means primarily to view firsthand, as if you were to see one car run a stoplight and crash into another. The verb may then become a noun as you go to court to tell what you have seen; you have become "a witness." That process of telling is central to Christianity. Jesus said, "You will be my witnesses in Jerusalem, in all Judea and Samaria, and to the ends of the earth" (Acts 1:8). Shortly after, the disciples became and did just that; on the day of Pentecost, they poured out into the streets, inspired by the Spirit, proclaiming what happened on Easter. Peter declares, "This Jesus God raised up, and of that all of us are witnesses" (Acts 2:32). From the Christian view, then, to witness is not merely to see, but to tell forth— specifically to view and to declare the mighty works of God.

Isn't that what happens at weddings? Everything is so lovely, so loving, that guests go forth reflecting on and talking about what they have seen. They gush about what a wonderful service it was, how beautiful the church, how fun the reception. At its center, so often and so rightly, stand the bride and groom and their love for each other. That is what people tend to proclaim most of all, having witnessed firsthand their commitment of love as husband and wife.

And at the heart of that, as we will continue to see, is the love of God—the same love that brought Jesus from the grave. We gather to witness another act of love by God.

Second, we gather together to "bless" this union.

Surely the Prayer Book "misspeaks." It is God who blesses. Oh yes! But God chooses to bless, among other means, *through* the Church. God's community of faith conveys its sacramental blessing through its ordained representative who is set apart through the power of the Holy Spirit by the Church. So the Church is actually a vehicle of God's grace. Marriage, as we shall see, also can be such a vehicle.

The congregation blesses in a second sense. Surrounding the bride and groom are family and friends, many or few, all sharing their own love, good wishes, prayers, and joys. Their presence, prayers, and support become other forms of blessing which are hardly less important.

...the joining together...

This is the third key element of a meaningful phrase. Note how ambiguous it is, never saying precisely *who* does the joining. For that, we wait until page 428 of the Prayer Book liturgy; for now, we can wonder about what is happening.

How did the couple meet? What twists and turns did their relationship take? Think back to how they grew up, what shaped their personalities, what inspired their interests, what molded their values, all of which influenced the two people who fell in love with each other and decided to marry. Every couple bring to the altar two stories which intertwine.

If you contemplate them aright, they become a story of God's activity in two people's lives, introducing, nudging, guiding, maybe even pushing them together when a nudge didn't work. Now they come before him to profess their love and commitment. They formally ratify what God has been doing for them and with them and through them all along.

...this man and this woman...

Have you encountered someone who claims to "love everyone"? Nice sentiment, maybe genuine. But love becomes real when it turns away from a warm, mushy abstraction and turns specific. True love involves how you regard *this* child, how you treat *that* man or woman. In marriage, one individual commits himself/herself to another unique person: very specific, very real. It is comparable in its small way to the specific, real, and very great example of God's love manifested in the person of Jesus, the "Word made flesh."

...in Holy Matrimony.

At last we reach the sentence's long-awaited payday. "Matrimony" is a medieval English word describing either the act of marrying or the relationship which results from it.[22] The key modifier "holy" means that both the act and the relationship are sanctified, offered to God.

What we engage in, then, differs from what happens at the city courthouse. Yes, God's power can work there as well as within a church. So we do recognize civil marriages, even providing a form for their subsequent blessing (BCP 434–435). Nonetheless, we gather intentionally before God to witness and bless the union of a man and a woman who, in God's name and within the Christian community, aim at leading a married life dedicated not only to each other but also to God. They invite the Lord of all the earth to become a full participant in their marriage.

The bond and covenant of marriage was established by God in creation...

In another sentence full of meaning, we learn the origin and nature of marriage. It all derives from God, who, we find, instituted it in the first place.

"Established by God in creation" refers to Genesis 2:4–9, 15–24, verses which constitute one of the suggested readings for later in the service. Genesis tells of Adam and Eve and their union in Eden before they got into trouble over fruit. From the outset, marriage between the two sorts of beings created in the likeness of God is a fundamental aspect of human life. Nothing could be more natural nor more basic. God planted marriage in creation along with grasses and trees and humanity itself. It is therefore a fundamental part of God's creative activity, then, and ever since. Marriage creates a new unit of society, as God intended ("Therefore a man leaves his father and his mother and clings to his wife, and they become one flesh," Genesis 2:24). Also, since one of its purposes is "the procreation of children," it actively engages human beings in the creative process. Of that, more later.

What God established was a "bond and covenant." These are heavily laden words. A "bond" is a link of great strength. It can be put to two very different uses. One is to imprison, like the bonds that shackle a prisoner to a cell wall. Another is to meld together like a "bonding agent" used in constructing a home or building a model airplane to unify two distinct materials as one. Wags at the bachelor's party may tease the groom with connotations of imprisonment, but marriage connotes the second sense instead. In conjoining two people as one, marriage actually liberates each to become something far greater than either could attain on his or her own.

The word "covenant" holds even richer meaning. In legal parlance, "covenant" and "contract" stand close together. Both denote a mutual agreement between two or more parties. A car buyer signs a contract to pay a frightful amount of money to purchase a particular vehicle, which the dealer must then deliver in the agreed-upon condition. They consent, in a way which is legal and public. But this contract tends to fit the one-time situation in which the goals, obligations, and desired outcome are clear, without implying any relationship beyond the terms specified. On the other hand, "covenant" suggests an ongoing tie of a long duration. A "covenant which runs with the land," for example, might be written into a land deed which says that the property cannot be developed. Goals of the relationship are clear and the commitment is mutual, but how it will be lived out is shrouded in uncertainty, even as it is guided by mutual commitment.[23]

This legal notion begins to suggest the religious importance of the term. "Covenant" implies a deep, abiding agreement which establishes an association between two parties, one of whom is usually God. The Prayer Book defines the term as "a relationship initiated by God, to which a body of people responds in faith" (BCP 846). The Bible is full of covenants. For example:

- God's covenant with the earth in the days of Noah, the symbol of which is the rainbow (Genesis 9);
- God's covenant with Abraham, giving him the land of Canaan and promising innumerable descendants (beginning in Genesis 15);

- The covenant with the people of Israel, given by the God who brought them out of Egypt and signified by the Ten Commandments (beginning in Exodus 24);
- The covenant Joshua renewed as the people entered the promised land (Joshua 24);
- The "new covenant" which Jesus proclaimed at the Last Supper, which is manifested by his own death and resurrection (see Luke 22:20).[24]

All these depict a God who chooses to relate to his people. Covenants also characterize marriage: a contract involving a legal partnership, but vastly more, an abiding, faithful relationship between two mutually committing parties. As with marriage, solemn ceremonies initiated covenants such as Abraham's (his covenants with God, e.g., Genesis 15:12–21; also his covenants with other people, e.g., with Abimelech, Genesis 21:25–31).

Covenants furthermore mark the start of relationships in terms that will guide and govern what happens thereafter. They set down the rights and responsibilities of each, often in broad and lofty ideals that can inspire as time and events progress well beyond the point of inception. A job description crafted at the start of employment guides in mundane language what happens long after. Someone joining the armed forces makes a solemn pledge to defend the Constitution; and this vow, together with the experience that follows, may prove to become a defining moment in his or her life as a citizen.

A new President enters into a kind of civic covenant with the people of the United States. Amid the ritualistic formalities of the inauguration, he may also redefine this covenant in ways that meet the challenges of the day and even enter the national soul. Phrases from inaugural speeches of Lincoln ("with malice toward none, with charity for all") and Kennedy ("ask not what your country can do for you")—phrases which were intended to articulate the aspirations for a term of office—have been incorporated into our tacit collective understanding of what we strive to become as a society. Biblical covenants, even more, were events of enormous consequence long remembered and often cited as a means of calling people to renew basic relationships, promises, duties, and hopes.

They were undertaken, too, at the outset of new events. Abraham's receiving and accepting God's promise, which led him to resettle in the land of Canaan, was ratified by a covenant that foretold of his offspring (Genesis 12, 15). The Sinai covenant came before the Israelites entered the land of promise. So covenants can mark a new venture, as its participants forge into unknown territory heartened by the confidence they derive from the covenant, their God, and each other.

In this light, marriage suggests a promised land of its own.

There is one more covenant of note: the "new covenant" in the blood and person of Jesus. His death and resurrection bring for Christians a "new exodus" into the ultimate promised land of God's kingdom, as we sing on Easter:

> Come ye faithful, raise the strain of triumphant gladness!
> God hath brought his Israel into joy from sadness:
> loosed from Pharaoh's bitter yoke Jacob's sons and daughters,
> led them with unmoistened foot through the Red Sea waters.[25]

Marriage, then, becomes, not only a new promised land, but a venture into the very kingdom of God that Jesus inaugurates in the new covenant of his resurrection. As a result, Holy Matrimony proclaims Easter and celebrates new life, as we shall see increasingly. Seen in that light, commitment—especially lifelong commitment—is anything but enslaving, as cynics would have it; in fact, it liberates a person (or, in this case, two) to enter a fullness of life not otherwise possible.

The next phrase signals the fact of this new life:

...and our Lord Jesus Christ adorned this manner of life by his presence and first miracle at a wedding in Cana of Galilee.

Jesus was himself a wedding guest, as John 2:1–11 describes:

> On the third day there was a wedding in Cana of Galilee, and the mother of Jesus was there. Jesus and his disciples had also been invited to the wedding. When the wine gave out, the mother of Jesus said to him, "They have no wine." And Jesus said to her, "Woman, what concern is that to you and to me? My hour has not yet come." His mother said to the servants, "Do whatever he tells you." Now standing there were six stone water jars for the Jewish rites of

purification, each holding twenty or thirty gallons. Jesus said to them, "Fill the jars with water." And they filled them up to the brim. He said to them, "Now draw some out, and take it to the chief steward." So they took it. When the steward tasted the water that had become wine, and did not know where it came from (though the servants who had drawn the water knew), the steward called the bridegroom and said to him, "Everyone serves the good wine first, and then the inferior wine after the guests have become drunk. But you have kept the good wine until now." Jesus did this, the first of his signs, in Cana of Galilee, and revealed his glory; and his disciples believed in him.

First, notice that the opening words, "on the third day," foreshadow an even greater happening "on the third day "—Jesus' resurrection.

Second, note the locale: a wedding, with his mother and disciples. The celebration becomes the setting for Jesus to work his very first miracle. There, amid family and friends, he changes water into wine.

This is a story of transformation. As with everything Jesus does, it signifies far more than the act itself. Jesus is no oenophile demanding the best wine even if he must work miracles to have it! Rather, as the first words hint at something greater, so the entire incident foreshadows what will happen as Jesus emerges through the gospel as the one who transforms what *is* into what *will be*, by the grace and power of God made manifest even in the midst of something so ordinary as a wedding.

So this is not really a story about weddings alone, but about the kingdom of God. The setting may be incidental. And maybe not. For this is an event that Jesus "adorned." He doesn't merely "decorate" it in the common sense of adding beauty to something. The definition is more basic and goes much further, pertaining to an event which Jesus, by his very presence, burnished with honor and splendor.[26]

And, clearly, the Jesus of John's gospel chose this particular setting to work his first miracle of transformation. For marriage can transform two individuals in ways that they cannot otherwise attain, all by the power of God. It is not the *only* way God transforms mortals—we must repeatedly remember that God does not call everyone to this state of life—but it is one way; and it is one which

Jesus "adorned" by his presence. He blesses not only the marriage he visited, but marriage in general. And matrimony becomes a means he uses to work his transforming power—not on wine, but on people.

Now for another sentence packed full of meaning:

It signifies to us the mystery of the union between Christ and his Church, and Holy Scripture commends it to be honored among all people.

The very word "signifies" signifies much. At its root is the word "sign." What are implications of marriage being a *sign*?

First, consider some familiar signs. One sort conveys little more than information, like "Massachusetts welcomes you," posted at the state border. Other signs are meant to provoke a response. A red octagon with white letters prompts a driver to press the brakes when reaching an intersection, whereas one with golden arches starts either one's stomach or one's children growling for a hamburger and fries.

There is another kind of sign, one that in my town says, "Lexington City Limits." Living on one side of that sign means voting for one set of officials at a given polling place, paying taxes at one rate to one government, sending the children to one set of schools and either having trash picked up or hauling it away yourself, all of which is different from living on the other side of the border it demarcates. The sign signifies a distinction in day-to-day reality.

The Church relies heavily on signs we call "sacraments." The Prayer Book defines these as "outward and visible signs of inward and spiritual grace, given by Christ as sure and certain means by which we receive that grace" (BCP 857). Like the city limits sign, these designate a shift in reality. Life is somehow different on the other side of sacramental signs. But unlike what we see beside a road, these actually bring that reality about by bestowing the grace of God upon a person or a couple. The "outward and visible signs" may be as common as water, or bread and wine, or husband and wife; but the inward and spiritual grace brings heaven itself to us. God transforms the ordinary, using common stuff of food and drink, woman and man, so that the ordinary becomes nothing less than a living sample of heaven.

Is the totality of this new reality fulfilled at that moment? No, not any more than the life of a baby at birth. Nonetheless, that child is fully alive, and the life is vividly real even if all but a day of it lies ahead in promise. Of course, much depends on how fully the person chooses to live out that new life; but the life has begun. Likewise, in sacraments the grace is bestowed, the life begun or renewed or started anew in a dynamic of God and faith and people.

Sacraments bring God's grace to us. They also make a demand— the obligation to respond in keeping with what is being offered, to live into that grace in such a way as to discover the measure of the joys and the strength which they also bring. The baby's life has begun, but that life takes on real meaning and purpose and joy as the child responds and interacts more and more to the people and world and, ultimately, the God who gives life itself. Similarly, a couple discover the nature of marriage as they enter more and more fully into its heights and depths.

Holy Matrimony, then, is a sign of God's grace. Often numbered among the seven traditional sacraments—the last one to be added to the list[27]—marriage is officially termed a "sacramental rite" in the Episcopal Church because it is "not necessary for all persons in the same way that Baptism and the Eucharist are" (BCP 860). Nonetheless, it conveys a grace and signifies a reality for the two people and those around them in a way that nothing else can. And on the wedding day, it is no less real for having only just begun. As they live into it, they discover the measure of joys and strengthening power which this outward and visible sign can bring.

Then what is that reality? "It signifies the mystery of the union between Christ and his Church." The phrase originates in Ephesians 5:32, a passage about marriage that compares that relationship to one of the Lord with his people.

This concept offers a way into understanding this mystery. We might ponder how Christ relates to his people. I think the easiest way of doing that is to recall how Jesus treated others as recorded in the Bible.

Hence, an exercise: on a piece of paper, jot down all the adjectives you can imagine that describe how Jesus treated those he encountered. It might help to visualize him traveling about Israel, and what he did along the way; then heading to Jerusalem and the sorts of things he said to his disciples; finally, in his last days, confronted by Pilate, dying on the cross, and at last raised from the dead and returning to meet his followers. Was he loving? Compassionate? What else?

What do you come up with?

Over the years, every couple preparing for marriage with me have answered this question. You can profit from their experience by turning to the notes at the end of this book. I hope that you can add to their list; for the list could be nearly endless.[28]

Now, review the items on your list, however many or few they may be, asking another question: How many of these qualities or adjectives apply to a good marriage?

Chances are that the figure is close to one hundred per cent.

In other words, the qualities that describe how Jesus dealt with others also describe how husband and wife ideally treat each other.

No coincidence.

To put the matter bluntly, the qualities which ideally prevail between husband and wife are those of Christ himself. These are qualities which should prevail among all people. We hope they will especially abide in this most intimate and intense of human relationships.

When they do, plenty of clichés take on genuine meaning: that the marriage "is made in heaven"; that it becomes "a little bit of heaven," or "heaven on earth." Above all, sharing the qualities of Jesus with each other means that husband and wife become Christ to the other. As they offer love and compassion, nurture and support, challenge yet also trust, they literally bring home what Jesus showed to those about him. They embody Christ's love; or, to use a theologically laden term, they "incarnate" the love of Jesus, the one called "Emmanuel" ("God with us"), who in St. John's words "was made flesh, and dwelt among us...full of grace and truth" (John 1:14). From this view, then, Holy Matrimony is one means by which Jesus continues his work and extends his love by being present through and with his people in our world and day. And this is what the husband and wife are sharing. They, ordinary people that they are, become agents of God in his ongoing work of transforming the world, such that their relationship becomes truly extraordinary. They even "represent Christ and his Church," which is precisely how the Church defines ministry (BCP 855).

This is why marriage never involves man and woman alone. Nor does it involve only them and their children, nor parents and friends and the congregation witnessing the vows, nor just the wider society of which they are a part. The circle instead embraces the entire kingdom of God, for husband and wife together become participants in the divine covenant of God through Christ, a "missionary station" for the work of Jesus, a franchise of the kingdom, a foretaste of heaven, a "haven of blessing and peace," as we will soon pray. Whatever metaphor you choose, the marriage can reflect on earth the nature of heaven itself.

No wonder, then, that the Prayer Book Exhortation reminds us that "Holy Scripture commends it to be honored among all people." This phrase, derived from Hebrews 13:4, is one of many biblical passages that "commend" marriage; a few others are listed on page 426 of the Prayer Book as options for the reading(s) at the wedding itself. Of these, among the most powerful is Genesis 2:24, which Jesus cites in Matthew 19:5–6, a passage so potent that the officiant quotes it in pronouncing man and woman as husband and wife (BCP 428).

This first pithy paragraph of "The Exhortation" lays out the central meaning of Holy Matrimony. It sets forward themes that we will encounter repeatedly in the service—and, ideally, that the couple will encounter in their life together.

Now we can move on to explore the very reasons for marriage.

Earliest Books of Common Prayer set forth three main reasons for marriage: for perpetuating the human race (recalling Genesis 1:28) within the framework of God's grace (Ephesians 4:6); for "a remedy against sin, and to avoid fornication, that such persons as have not the gift of continency might marry..."; and for the "mutual society, help, and comfort" they offer each other.[29] The current Prayer Book accentuates clearly positive rationales for marriage:

The union of husband and wife in heart, body, and mind...

This union is the most complete, most intimate relationship any two human beings can have. It is a union in multiple senses.

First, it unites two people more fully than anything else ever can. In sexual intercourse, their bodies "become one flesh" in an almost literal way. But sex brings the pair together more than physically. A British theologian observes, "The sexual act is seen as 'the outward and visible sign of an inward spiritual grace,' that is to say, not as a merely biological act but as the expression of a personal bond between the partners."[30] Bodily union promotes and expresses an emotional unity, in the heart as romance grows but also as the hassles of coping with new jobs or deciding who washes the dishes brings them ever more closer. When children start arriving, they must come to be "of one mind" on matters ranging from who gets up for early-morning feedings to whatever curfews to set on teenagers, from which church to attend to what job to take and which house to buy. However, "union" never means "uniformity." Each remains a distinctive person, with gifts, ideas, and an individual personality. "Union" does, though, suggest a cohesion which binds the two together in every way possible.

In developing a partnership in marriage, each individual may find life coming together in a new way. One factor is simply being loved which, vastly more than providing "warm fuzzies" and good feelings, affirms a person on a daily basis as nothing else can. Another is in drawing from each other's strengths, learning from each other. To take a small example, my wife is by nature a terrific organizer. I am the opposite—or *was*, for over the years I have begun to practice what she does all the time. Not only have we benefitted as a twosome from her skills, I have also picked up a few of them myself. As a couple mature through this union as a partnership, each individual flourishes as well. In practical, emotional, and spiritual ways, the whole exceeds the sum of its parts.[31]

For all the great potential, there is also particular danger in marriage. The very intimacy which can make this union so strong also exposes each partner to the greatest vulnerability. Not just physically do husband and wife stand naked before each other. They "know" each other in the biblical sense of sexual intimacy but in nearly every other way too—the fears, the soft spots, the passions, the traits. Weaknesses and failures hidden to the world may be known only to the spouse. Often a wife perceives in her husband what no one else (including her husband) can see—and vice-versa.

Such powerful knowledge can wound deeply. Each is totally vulnerable to the other (Latin students will recall that "vulnerable" means "able to be wounded"). But through love and trust, that very vulnerability allows the union to grow even stronger.

...is intended by God for their mutual joy...

I ask couples preparing for marriage, "Are you happy?" They always answer, "Yes!" Good thing, too, for many reasons—and one is that they are fulfilling thereby an intention of God.

Talking of marriage as an "outpost of the kingdom of Heaven" may make it sound like some onerous burden that two people carry. Maybe so, but only in the name of one who said, "My yoke is easy, and my burden is light" (Matthew 11:30). Marriage should be as joyous as the kingdom promises. When it is, it becomes all the more a sign of Jesus' presence.

We may think of "ministry" as a missionary journey far away to what Paddington Bear called "darkest Peru." Serving God, we think, involves feeding the hungry at the local soup kitchen, or building houses with Habitat for Humanity to help the homeless, or teaching church school, or becoming ordained. Yes, it is those things and countless more. But serving God can also be as simple and as near at hand as taking joy as husband and wife. Of such, too, is the kingdom of God.

...for the help and comfort given one another in prosperity and adversity...

Any marriage faces good times and bad. Such is life. The Prayer Book always keeps before us those realities that everyone faces in living in this world ("for richer for poorer, in sickness and in health," BCP 427). In marriage, partners strive to confront the good and the bad together as a union that they have become; and when they do, they find their bonds strengthened all the more.

You might recall some moments of great difficulty that you have faced. What effect did it have on your relationship with your betrothed (or spouse, as the case may be)? What about times of great joy? Looking back on those experiences, you may have found "comfort" in more senses than one, for that term denotes not simply a soothing quality but also a tone of strength and encouragement that earlier Prayer Books had very much in mind.[32]

...and, when it is God's will, for the procreation of children and their nurture in the knowledge and love of the Lord.

God, we believe, creates all things. "Procreation" suggests the creative process of engendering or bringing forth. Human procreation perpetuates the race and extends into a new generation the activity of the Creator God who commended it to Adam and Eve and all who follow them (Genesis 1:28). Many a new parent looks with wondrous awe at the new life he or she helped bring into the world, vividly conscious of sharing in what God does.

That, of course, is just the beginning.

I once met a lady who, years before on her wedding day, announced to her groom that they were going to have twelve children. (Quickly—if you haven't done so already—talk with your betrothed/spouse about how many you might wish!) And so it happened. Their offspring numbered an even dozen. Problem was, they were great at procreating, not so great at nurturing; rumor has it that she went at one with a kitchen knife. Remarkably, some turned out to be fine people; God's grace can work wonders. But parents have the job of helping that grace along—again, making real and embodying that love he shows us.

Procreating may be the fun part, but what follows is the more important. Sociological data are confirming what most societies have long recognized, that it takes two—father and mother, at the very least, in a stable, committed relationship—for the fullest well-being of children.[33] Nurturing is the greater challenge and ultimately, as any good parent knows, even more "fun" in a rewarding, long-lasting way.

Notice that this is nurture "in the knowledge and love of the Lord." As Holy Matrimony transcends mere marriage, so rearing children within the context of Holy Matrimony moves beyond ordinary, worldly nurture. It embraces far more, which is to bring children to know and love God. In the home, what the Church calls "Christian education" and even "evangelism" take meaning through the very process of family life. Notice the commitment of parents when a child is baptized (BCP 302). At its best, the life of the family arises unselfconsciously out of the commitments and covenants that have already begun in Holy Matrimony.

Therefore marriage is not to be entered into unadvisedly or lightly, but reverently, deliberately, and in accordance with the purposes for which it was instituted by God.

No wonder, then, that the Church asks—even insists—that a couple pray about and ponder what they are doing, for their own sake above all, but also for their family's (present and future), their community's, and even for the sake of God.

But reverence and deliberation do not preclude joy! On the contrary, "mutual joy" counts as one basic aim. It comes about best, we have discovered over the past 2,000 years, when two people understand what they are about so that they can commit themselves to each other and to reaching, as much as possible, the ideals which marriage holds forth to them.

When this becomes a couple's goal, they are caught up in an even vaster ideal. For marriage both reflects and contributes to some ultimate schemes of God.

The Bible lets us know what those plans might be. According to the Letter to the Ephesians, Jesus Christ revealed a divine design for the entire universe.

> With all wisdom and insight [God] has made known to us the mystery of his will, according to his good pleasure that he set forth in Christ, as a plan for the fullness of time, to gather up all things in him, things in heaven and things on earth. (Ephesians 3:8–10)

Christ, then, discloses the very meaning of creation. God's purpose is to unite all things under the headship of the Son and the Fatherhood of God. Jesus reveals this by his very nature, for unity marks the fundamental relationship of the Father and the Son in indissoluble communion (see John 10:14–15, 17:21). He also discloses this through the ideal of the Church—Christ's people (see John 17:23). With that in mind, the last Collect* of the Church's year prays,

---

The ancient notion of a "collect" (COL'-lect) is of a prayer which summarizes the various intentions of the congregation, as if to gather the silent petitions of the people and raise them to the Almighty.

Almighty and everlasting God, whose will it is to restore
all things in your well-beloved Son, the King of kings and Lord of
lords: Mercifully grant that the peoples of the earth, divided
and enslaved by sin, may be freed and brought together
under his most gracious rule.... (BCP 236)

Earliest Christians began to perceive that all that Jesus did served
this ultimate purpose. In his teaching and preaching and miracles, in
his calling of the disciples and in his visiting the outcast and scorned,
and supremely in his death and resurrection, Jesus served to bring
people together with each other and with God. As Paul marveled,
Christ ended the separation between Jew and Greek, slave and free,
male and female (Galatians 3:28; see also Colossians 3:11). Returning
to Ephesians, we read that "now in Christ Jesus you who once were far
off have been brought near by the blood of Christ. For he is our peace;
in his flesh he has made both groups into one and has broken down the
dividing wall, that is, the hostility between us" (Ephesians 2:13–14).
All become one in Christ, in the kingdom of God (Colossians 1:13).

As these first Christians also understood, the Church plays a
crucial role in Christ's unifying work. After all, Jew and Greek, slave
and free, male and female all become one within the Body of Christ.
Masters and slaves would partake of the same holy loaf as brothers
and sisters in Christ. True, they had their differences (see Acts 6:1 and
Acts 11 for two examples). They also had their distinctivenesses, but
these in turn made them stronger when functioning together. This
was Paul's point in his image of a body whose individual members
are as distinctive as a foot and a hand; but working together, they
allow the body to function effectively (1 Corinthians 12:14–26).

The Church, then, became something of a foretaste of an even
greater unity to come. Every week, celebrating the Eucharist gave
Christians a sense of Christ's presence and their oneness with each
other and him even as they looked forward to that day when he
would return and make that unity perfect. What the earliest
Christians perceived, we share and find still to be true.

Marriage fits into that overall plan of our Lord. It unites two
people in love. Whether they come from different continents or the
same block, they always emerge from distinctive backgrounds,
perspectives, ways, and customs; yet in Christ, they become one.

Furthermore, as spouses mature with each other, their union of distinctivenesses becomes ever deeper. "Unity" never means a uniformity so total that one becomes a clone of the other. Instead, each retains an identity so that something more mysterious evolves, in which two distinctive individuals abide in what we pray will be an ever increasing harmony. As they do, in their small way they show forth on earth what God aims for the cosmos.

In the end, as the Book of Revelation concludes, the Church as the people of God shall become what John the Divine refers to—how pertinently for us—as the "bride of Christ."

> And I saw the holy city, the new Jerusalem, coming down out of heaven from God, prepared as a bride adorned for her husband. And I heard a loud voice from the throne saying, "See, the home of God is among mortals. He will dwell with them as their God; they will be his peoples, and God himself will be with them. (Revelation 21:2–3)[34]

That is how a mystery concludes, a mystery we experience right now (among other ways) in marriage. By "mystery" I do not mean a murder solved in an hour of television, but, rather, something beyond our capacity fully to comprehend. It is like looking ahead while walking through mists of a foggy day. Some shapes seem rather clear; others are blurred while still more stand beyond our ability to see; yet what little we can see hints at even bigger things to come. Christ has revealed much to us. We can begin to detect the nature of his redeeming, reconciling work. We know the direction he is taking us, even if we cannot discern precisely where or how. And we can sense that marriage is very much part of that journey and work and plan. For marriage is itself a mystery, an element of the even greater mystery of God's plan for the universe he created.

Thus, Holy Matrimony truly is a sign of the kingdom of God, on earth as it is in heaven.

In its ideal, then, Christian marriage takes a wide variety of fundamental themes of our faith and brings them to life:

- Creation: The God who made all things calls two people into a new relationship, uniquely their own. Entering a relationship rooted in creation (Genesis 1:27–2:24, Matthew 19:1–11), they are themselves a new creation (see Galatians 6:15), one which restores in a sense what God originally intended. Like Adam and Eve before the apple, they will be to the other "naked, and...not ashamed" (Genesis 2:25)—naked physically, emotionally, even spiritually. And, depending on God's will, from this creation, from moments of nakedness, new life—or lives—may also emerge.

- Incarnation: Husband and wife "enflesh" love for each other, not just literally as the term "making love" implies of intercourse, but even more as they share the qualities of the Lord Jesus toward one another and those about them.

- Sacrifice: Becoming like Christ means, among other things, the surrender of self, following the Lord's example (Philippians 2:5–11). One image of this self-sacrifice is baptism. Another is marriage. The left hand (to borrow Paul's image of the body) must know what the right hand is doing to accomplish anything, which means giving up some of its independence. Committing to another means giving up a degree of freedom for the sake of something greater—thereby discovering the new life of grace.

- Redemption and grace: A senior bishop once reflected, "Though I'd been to seminary and was ordained for a few years, I never understood what was meant by God's grace until I was married; and then I found that my wife loved me for who I was. Then I knew, and it has made all the difference." Christ makes us new people. Marriage can help.

- Resurrection: In often dramatic ways, marriage signifies a new life. He had a checkered past, she endured a dreadful relationship before they found each other; each in their way suffered versions of crucifixion before they discovered new life. Together, they were wonderful. So was their marriage. And boundless was their gratitude to each other, and to God.

- Ministry and Service: To "represent Christ and his Church" is the Catechism's basic definition of ministry (BCP 855). As two people share those qualities which we find both in Jesus and in healthy marriages, they are "representing Christ" to their children, parents, families, friends, and all those around them...just by being themselves!

- Sanctification: "Be perfect, as your heavenly Father is perfect" (Matthew 5:48). A tall order. But marriage helps. For as a couple grow in those qualities of Christ, each becomes more and more like Jesus, the Son of God. Through marriage, then, the Holy Spirit can help lead each and both into greater and greater holiness, which, for a Christian, is being like Christ— in Paul's words "conformed to the image of [God's] son" (Romans 8:29).

- Fulfillment of God's Kingdom: With that kind of growth, and that sort of relationship with each other and with the Lord, a couple can begin to perceive what God intends for all people. They can detect what God has in mind for the cosmic order, even as they share in his work of bringing about that unity in Jesus Christ. How they do that may seem so very ordinary—by living out their vows in faithfulness to each other and to God, by growing in love and joy, by being happy, by sharing with each other and with those about them. But in so doing they can savor a foretaste of what will come, fully and completely, for all of God's people.

So, the mystery unfolds—and that which seems so common on the surface becomes in the hands of God nothing less than truly extraordinary.

Betrothal

$\mathcal{M}$arriage always marks a new beginning. Inevitably, though less evidently, it also marks a departure—an end to childhood (for many), the leaving of the home and what counselors call "the family of origin," a dramatic change in primary loyalties and relationships for parents, siblings, friends and children, if there may be, along with the two themselves. So it was at the outset; Genesis declares, "Therefore a man leaves his father and his mother and clings to his wife, and they become one flesh" (Genesis 2:24). No wonder so many stereotypical mothers use such large quantities of tissue!—for on many levels this is an emotional time.

To mark these departures definitively, it is crucial to ascertain that the proceedings are legal and that all is agreeable to the key parties involved. This is the essence of the next section, traditionally known as the "Betrothal," when formal pledges to enter into matrimony are exchanged.

In medieval England, this bit of necessary business took place outside the church door, as if to acknowledge all secular and public legalities before the couple proceeded into sacred space. Reformation custom, however, posited a different emphasis by holding the betrothal in "the body of the church" in the explicit presence of "their friends and neighbours." This had the implicit effect of both blessing the necessary secular protocols and of underscoring the nature of marriage as a corporate, ecclesial event. Later in the service, they would move from the nave to "the Lord's Table."[35] The custom of many parishes follows this essential pattern, with the service through the Ministry of the Word occurring in the nave and the clergy and bridal party approaching the altar for the vows or blessing, though this movement is optional (BCP 437).

The Banns

Into this holy union N.N. and N.N. now come to be joined.
If any of you can show just cause why they may not lawfully be married, speak now; or else for ever hold your peace.

The opening exhortation, so brief to speak, so long to explain, lays out a Christian understanding of marriage within the context of the kingdom of God. It is lofty, idealistic, and general. God's kingdom, though, always becomes most real when it turns specific, having to do with *this* person or *that* couple.

So the priest gets specific:

Into this holy union N.N. and N.N. now come to be joined.

All that we have described is something *this* man, by name, and *this* woman, by name, will enter.

Recall baptism for a moment. Sponsors accompanied the candidate to the font and announced the person's name. Then, while pouring water onto or even immersing the person, the celebrant spoke the individual's name: "*N.*, I baptize you in the Name of the Father, and of the Son, and of the Holy Spirit" (BCP 307). If and when the baptized person was confirmed, the bishop spoke again the name: "Strengthen, O Lord, your servant *N.* with your Holy Spirit" (BCP 309 or 418). In rites which are highly personal though never individualistic, the community of faith rejoices in what God does anew for this particular child of his.

The celebrant now announces the names of those who face another activity instituted by God. For purposes of full identification, the celebrant uses their complete names. Hereafter, he will use their "given" names—the ones they used at baptism. (In light of the solemnity and seriousness of marriage, and because one element of marriage is a legal contract, now is not the time for nicknames.)

If any of you can show just cause why they may not lawfully be married, speak now; or else for ever hold your peace.

The point has come when bride and groom hold their breath: Who might object? And why?

Stories are told of what happens at this moment: the well-timed cough, the sound of a carefully-dropped hymnal echoing through the church. My favorite tells of the young man who, hearing the inexorable question, stands up in back of a huge church. "Excuse me," he says climbing over shocked pewmates. All eyes turn, wondering if this might be an old beau of the bride or a classmate of the groom with scandal to tell. The priest must stop, of course, while bride and groom peer at this interrupter. Making out his features, they look in bewilderment at who this intruder might be. At last he reaches the front, looks at the groom, looks at the bride, then exclaims, "Whoops!—wrong wedding" as he scampers out.

If someone objects, the officiant must pause and consider the objection.* A rejected suitor or memories of wild oats do not constitute grounds to stop the wedding. What might? Information that either of the couple is not of age, or that neither is baptized, or that one is married or insane—any "impediment" identified at the outset.

The query itself is a vestige of days before state-issued marriage licenses. Then, the banns and the question at the ceremony itself, which was and is always public, made sure that all was well. But with nothing to hide, a couple can appear confidently before God and the world knowing that neither objection nor tasteless joke can stand in their way to the altar.**

The Charge

No one speaks or even coughs. Bride, groom, and priest all exhale a sigh of relief. The priest now turns to the couple and asks essentially the same question of them:

> I require and charge you both, here in the presence of God,
> that if either of you know any reason why you may not be
> united in marriage lawfully, and in accordance with God's
> Word, you do now confess it. (BCP 424)

---

*I have heard of two approaches taken by priests who heard an objection raised at this point in the ceremony. In one case, the officiant took the objecting party, the bride and groom, and the parents of each into his study to hear what turned out to be an impediment sufficient enough to call off the wedding. In the other, the priest called for a chair, sat down, and heard the protest in front of the entire congregation. She then overruled the objection, asked ushers to escort the protester out, and proceeded with the ceremony.

**My associate once presided over a notorious wedding-that-wasn't. Family and friends, even members of the wedding party, believed the couple to be mismatched, ill-suited, and headed for disaster. They threatened to object. Technically, they had no grounds; and as it happened, they had no opportunity, for the brawl after the rehearsal dinner ended the entire fiasco. Anyone with sincere objections should voice them early and responsibly; and bride and groom should listen carefully. The wedding is not the place for last-minute protests, even though the opportunity for one must remain.

38   Bond and Covenant

The current Prayer Book eliminates the dire phrasing of earlier books ("as you will answer at the dreadful day of judgment when the secrets of all hearts shall be disclosed"[36]). Nonetheless, it conveys that this is serious stuff. Woman and man stand on the verge of something utterly awesome. After baptism, no commitment a person makes is greater or more permanent or farther-reaching. Each should have carefully pondered the question long before and all along. Any reservation (much less impediment) that came to mind already should have been explored, preferably together. Now, one last time, if they know any reason why not to proceed, they have one last chance to say so.

The Declaration of Consent

They know no reason why not. Accordingly, the celebrant asks them a positive question:

The Celebrant says to the woman

N., will you have this man to be your husband; to live together in the covenant of marriage? Will you love him, comfort him, honor and keep him, in sickness and in health; and, forsaking all others, be faithful to him as long as you both shall live?

The Woman answers

I will.

The Celebrant says to the man

N., will you have this woman to be your wife; to live together in the covenant of marriage? Will you love her, comfort her, honor and keep her, in sickness and in health; and, forsaking all others, be faithful to her as long as you both shall live?

The Man answers

I will.

In lean and eloquent language, the questions intertwine so many of the themes we have already explored and invite the woman and man to take on this state of life.

...will you have this man/woman to be your husband/wife?...

Millions of people exist whom the bride/groom have no reason *not* to marry; but only one stands nearby and before God whom the bride/groom has determined she/he *will* marry. So the celebrant addresses by name first the woman, then the man, and asks the solemn question if each will enter that sacred and awe-filled vocation of Holy Matrimony.

...to live together in the covenant of marriage?

The term "covenant" reappears. Its use here—replacing the phrase "holy estate of matrimony" of earlier Prayer Books—emphasizes the nature of the relationship as the Exhortation defined it, and as the next question will make even more specific.

Will you love him/her, comfort him/her, honor and keep him/ her?...

As I said earlier, some claim to "love everybody." Christians see beyond this sentimental impossibility. True love directs itself at the particular—*this* man, *this* woman, *this* child. Thereby, love moves beyond emotion to contend directly with all the joys and sorrows of immediate, day-by-day encounters. Love of this sort transcends the romance of candles and lace to confront the realities of job moves, vacation and retirement, of passionate sex and possible indiscretions, of personal talents but also of personal failures, of the very best a person can be but, potentially, also the very worst.

"Love" is the first of the four verbs the celebrant asks each to live by. The second, "comfort," is one we encountered in the Exhortation. The term derives from the Latin root *fort-*, as in "fortitude." Instead of connoting cozy quilts and warm fires, it implies a power which braces and strengthens and upholds the other. If making the spouse "comfortable" accompanies it, then so much the better!

"Honor" is the third verb in the pledge. I read somewhere of a wife who looked at her husband of some years and asked, "Do you love me?" Without glancing from his newspaper, he answered, "yes." She asked again, "But do you *love* me?" "What kind of question is that?" he demanded, then realized she needed more. "Yes, you know I love you." She said, "then why don't you *value* me?"

To "honor" is to offer respect and esteem, treating another with courtesy and consideration in a way that exalts and ennobles the person. Blessed is the couple who mutually admire each other.

We ordinarily think of the final verb "keep" in terms of permanence; and that surely befits the matrimonial pledge of lifelong fidelity. Its etymology reveals another sense, equally fitting, of taking care of or upholding something or someone—one who "keeps" one's word; or one who keeps books or a diary or office hours; or those famous shepherds who keep "watch over their flocks by night" (Luke 2:8). To "keep" in this sense connotes maintaining ongoing care and concern. This, too, each pledges.

...in sickness and in health...

The Prayer Book holds before us a down-to-earth, vivid, unsentimentalized nature of love. And how real it is! For marriage is not an endless honeymoon during which all is perfect by worldly standards. Nevertheless, in confronting together the sorrows of life, in reveling together in its joys, the couple find a greater strength than could otherwise be possible. Their whole is greater than the sum of the parts, for they derive strength from each other and from the One who promised, "Where two or three are gathered in my name, I am there among them" (Matthew 18:20).

...forsaking all others, be faithful to him/her as long as you both shall live?

Here's a double whammy: "forsaking all others" and "be faithful" for life. Demanding, but this is the biblical tradition of marriage. Two of the Ten Commandments apply, "Thou shalt not commit adultery" and "Thou shalt not covet thy neighbor's wife." Jesus teaches faithfulness in marriage as indicated by its permanence (Matthew 19:3–9). From an even larger view, marriage reflects the faithfulness of Jesus himself, an image of the divine commitment to God's people.

Each answers, "I will." Not "I do." The question asks their *willingness* to wed, anticipating the marriage itself will follow. That's when they "do."

Consent is crucial. In earlier days, it mattered nearly above all else.[37] The fundamental reasoning is simple: There can be no true marriage against one's will. Success in marriage depends upon willingness to marry.

Then follows a question for all:

The Celebrant then addresses the congregation, saying

Will all of you witnessing these promises do all in your power to uphold these two persons in their marriage?

People   We will. (BCP 425)

In the presence of God also stand all sorts of family and friends of bride and groom: parents and grandparents, siblings and cousins, childhood chums, college classmates, fellow works from the job. Perhaps only two stand by; perhaps they number in the hundreds. These are people who have shaped the bride and groom as individuals and, perhaps, the two of them as a couple. In one pew may sit the friend who introduced one to the other (maybe through that most miraculous of events, the successful blind date). Nearby, in the wedding party, is one who listened to tales of hot passion or cold feet. Together they comprise a human host of witnesses who have helped in some way to shape or even to bring about the relationship now finding its fulfillment in matrimony. They also are part of this drama, for they are part of this couple's life—past, present, and future as well.

In turn, those people will themselves be affected by this marriage. A wedding marks a far-reaching change in relationships within the dynamic structure of family and friendships. Parents "gain a son/ daughter." Friends have already included this other person in their circle, or they have grown accustomed to the fact that loyalties have shifted and that their old buddy doesn't come around as much as before. A child by a previous marriage watches another person formally enter his parent's life—and his own. Marriage marks a dramatic change for them all.

The question which the celebrant puts to them is new to the 1979 Prayer Book (and, I think, a welcome addition). Imagine the effect on the couple if one set of parents, for instance, were lukewarm about these nuptials, or if one of their old friends was so bitterly opposed that she almost boycotted the service, or if their children by a previous marriage were trying up to the last minute to reunite their divorced parents. In ways great and small, ambivalence or opposition can undermine the marriage, sometimes eating away at it like a cancer, sometimes pounding it like a sledgehammer. Neither does any good for the couple.

On the other hand, active support from those around them can become a tremendous strength to wife and husband. The ongoing encouragement, the grandparents' assistance with children, the friendly advice, the voices of experience, the quiet prayers: there are countless ways that others lend their aid. For, if no marriage exists in isolation, but instead occurs within community, then the community can help a marriage to succeed.

The celebrant's question for the witnesses puts each person present very much on the line. It asks *"all* of you"—those who in all the world are closest to the couple—not only to put aside any opposition, but also to shun ambivalence in favor of active support for the decision which bride and groom are making.

There is more. In my understanding at least, those in the congregation answer not only for themselves, but for the entire Church of God throughout time and space. As at baptism—when the congregation makes the same promise for themselves and also for the entire body of Christ (which the baptismal candidate will be joining)—so, now, at marriage these witnesses serve as representatives of the whole Church.

That carries an important implication: The entire Church commits to support and uphold these two persons in their vocation of marriage. As a result, the couple should expect to be able to call upon the assistance of the Church whenever they need it. Should they encounter difficulty, they should feel free, for instance, to turn to a priest for pastoral support, whether or not they belong to the parish that priest serves; for they have been married within the community of faith which vastly transcends the particular site of their wedding. They are not merely married in "a church"; they are married in "the Church."

Of course, finding such help works best when the couple actively participate in the community of faith. What might that mean for them? Ideally, regularly attending worship, contributing time and talent as well as treasure, sharing in the fellowship of the parish, working in some way to build up the body of Christ to the glory of God—all those aspects that flow from fulfilling their baptismal vows as vibrant members of the Church.

Circumstances may make this simple response difficult. Especially, different religious backgrounds of husband and wife cause complexities which the couple should discuss explicitly with each other and with the priest who is overseeing their preparation for marriage. It is not a topic to avoid! Yet, out of it can emerge some creative solutions which, instead of tearing people apart (which can happen), brings them together. Religious practice, of course, should lie at the heart of the covenant.

The Presentation

There follows on page 425 of the Prayer Book a rubric that is basically a liturgical stage direction:

If there is to be a presentation or a giving in marriage,
it takes place at this time. See page 437.

By tradition, the father escorts his daughter down the aisle. In Prayer Book services going back to 1549, he would then "give" his daughter away, conforming to an even older tradition that daughters (and subsequently wives) were essentially pieces of property—not necessarily bought and sold outright (although the taking and receiving of marriage dowries amounted to much the same thing)—but legally conveyed, nonetheless, from one male to another.

Some brides wish to follow the traditional pattern. Others prefer a more contemporary expression. A father is not always around to escort his daughter; and some may wish a role for parents on both sides of the aisle. And some couples stand on their own, considering this gesture inappropriate for their situation.

To accommodate the variety, the Prayer Book provides for four different options (see rubrics under "Additional Directions," BCP 437):

- Who gives this woman to be married to this man?
- Who presents this woman to be married to this man?

These two options (either "giving" or "presenting" the woman) allow one or more from the bride's side to respond, "I do" or something similar.

- Who presents this woman and this man to be married to each other?

People, usually family, from the groom's side may join those from the bride's side in responding.

One option remains:

- Nothing. The giving/presentation is entirely optional, and nothing *need* be said at this point.

I leave it to the couple, especially the bride, to decide what best fits their situation.

The optional "presentation" may be followed by another option, a psalm, hymn, or anthem, after which the first portion of the ceremony comes to a close. We have established that the couple are ready, willing, and able to enter into the bond and covenant of marriage. We have invited the support of all those in the church, and all those of the Church—the body of Christ. And we have set forth the very nature of Holy Matrimony as a glorious act of God, a vocation to which these two are called, in love and by love, as they respond to God.

The stage is set for the next great act in this drama. But first comes a time to reflect on what that drama truly entails.

The Ministry of the Word

$\mathcal{G}$od, who has been in the background during our attention on bride and groom, now becomes our focus as we turn specifically to him in prayer and meditation.

Those who were married using Prayer Books prior to 1979 may be surprised by this section. It wasn't there. The Ministry of the Word is missing, not because the drafters of earlier Prayers Books considered the Bible unimportant, but because the first Prayer Books presumed that the then-familiar practice of embedding the marriage rite within the Sunday liturgy would continue. With this arrangement, the lessons and sermon, followed by the Holy Communion, were all integral parts of the ceremony, and the presence of the Christian community was guaranteed.[38] In the century following the first days of the Reformation, marriage and Eucharist became segregated from each other, not least because Communion was celebrated less frequently. The end result of these developments was to disengage the matrimonial rite from its traditional place within the context of the Ministry of the Word and the Ministry of the Sacrament of Holy Communion.

In our day, the separation may be reversing itself. Because of the current Prayer Book's emphasis upon the Eucharist in general, these historic connections with earlier Church practice have been restored to the marriage rite, so much so that it is no longer unheard of for weddings to occur during the regular Sunday morning service—complete with the Ministry of the Word and, usually, the Eucharist. The majority of weddings, of course, still are planned as events unto themselves and, therefore, tend to occur on any day other than Sunday. It is for these weddings that the new Prayer Book facilitates inclusion of the Eucharist. The rubric at the top of page 426 first introduces the list of suggested readings from scripture, then goes on to describe how these readings will be arranged "If there is to be a Communion." In this way, the rubric manages succinctly and matter-of-factly to place the marriage rite within the context of the Ministry of the Word that is so familiar to couples who attend Communion services regularly. For them, inclusion of Eucharist in their wedding may seem natural and, for some, perhaps even "essential." Conversely, for those who choose not to include Eucharist, the careful wording of the rubric will seem instructive but not prescriptive; nothing about the rubric suggests that their ceremony will be lessened in any way because of their decision.

While Communion truly is optional, note that the Ministry of the Word is mandatory. All weddings using the 1979 Prayer Book incorporate one or more readings from the Bible. In my experience, having the Word of God as an integral part of their wedding is a requirement which couples seem greatly to appreciate. Such is the importance and abiding appeal of the Bible.

The Collect for Marriage

The Celebrant then says to the people

> The Lord be with you.
> *People*   And also with you.

Let us pray.

> O gracious and everliving God, you have created us male and
> female in your image: Look mercifully upon this man and this
> woman who come to you seeking your blessing, and assist
> them with your grace, that with true fidelity and steadfast love
> they may honor and keep the promises and vows they make;
> through Jesus Christ our Savior, who lives and reigns with
> you in the unity of the Holy Spirit, one God, for ever and ever.
> *Amen.*

The collect above condenses some now-familiar themes: first, creation in general, male and female in particular, recalling the first two chapters of Genesis and the Exhortation's reference to what "was established by God"; second, the "grace" of God, a word which makes its first appearance here in the collect, but which also has been hinted at in the first paragraph of the Exhortation; third, faithfulness and love, as evidenced by the couple's Declaration of Consent.

The collect expresses again another insight. The man and woman "come to" God seeking his blessing. A few moments earlier, the celebrant announced that they "come now to be joined." By their choice, they present themselves before God to assume the remarkable responsibilities and opportunities which the joining together in marriage uniquely presents.

But neither they nor the multitude watching them are alone in this choice, for they are also responding to an ongoing activity of God.

Think for a moment about your own experience: How did you meet? What drew you to each other? What did you see in this person that aroused the thought of marriage?

Whenever I ask couples that question, invariably I discover fascinating answers. Sometimes the tale is as illogical as a miracle; sometimes the evolution is as orderly as if it had been planned all along. Yet that is the point: Whether miraculous or completely commonplace, the hand of God might well be perceived, nudging along, pushing here, holding back there, all in a quiet process that brings them to stand before him in joyous, nervous prayer.

In that prayer, they invoke the active participation of God within the marriage. The couple "come to" God "seeking [his] blessing." We ask God to "look mercifully" upon them and "assist them with [his] grace" to the end that they may "honor and keep the vows they make." So lofty and imposing and demanding are these vows that ultimately the only way the couple can uphold them through "sickness and health" and "better and worse" is by the help, the grace, of God. But, with God's help, these vows become—like any hard work well (if imperfectly) done—sheer delight.

The prayer concludes with the ascription "through Jesus Christ our Lord." Though standard form for collects—all our prayers and praises arise to the Father through what the Bible calls "our great high priest," Jesus[39]—this phrase holds special import, for at the heart of Holy Matrimony stands our Lord. As Savior, he also is the agent of creation (see John 1:3 and the Nicene Creed which states, "through him all things were made"), the one who "adorned" marriage, the miracle-worker (a role perhaps of special relevance, recognized by parents who exclaim, "It's just a miracle that he found someone so exactly right for him!"), the one who sent his Spirit to guide, bless, lead, and sustain his people and to gather us together as one into his resurrection. For marriage denotes new life; and that new life can become, above all, an expression—an "outward and visible sign"—of the new life in Christ.

Yet marriage is not just a new life which is to come. No, the blessing that the couple asks has already begun to happen. They would not be standing there, were it not for God. They have already started to be united as one. If so, the God that brought them together will bless them all the more for responding to what God so bluntly or so subtly has been inviting them to do and be. Already, the promise of God has begun to come true, even as so much more awaits.

The Lessons

Readings from the Holy Scripture follow next. This sequence of collect, lesson(s), and optional psalms parallels the pattern of the Holy Eucharist. No coincidence. By design, the rite of Holy Matrimony can fit neatly into the context of the sacrament of Christ's body and blood, if so desired (as it was done when the marriage rite routinely was performed within the regular Sunday worship). If no Eucharist is planned, hearing the biblical Word of God nonetheless becomes an integral part of every celebration of marriage.

I invite the bride and groom to choose the passages. The process of choosing, of looking up and considering each option, gives them time to reflect together on much that the Bible has to say about marriage, while also allowing them to personalize the service by emphasizing what seems best to articulate their understanding. I also invite them to ask family or friends to read the lessons, which is encouraged by the Prayer Book (BCP 422) for readings other than the Gospel lection.

Lections from the Old Testament and Apocrypha

Genesis 1:26–28 describes God's culminating act of creation in making humanity in his image, male and female, whom he blessed, instructed to "be fruitful and multiply," and gave dominion over the world.

Genesis 2:4–9, 15–24, a passage frequently mentioned already, summarizes the second creation story. It highlights the creation of man and woman in a way which emphasizes the interrelationship between them, especially as husband and wife.

Song of Solomon 2:10–13, 8:6–7 takes two passages from a book which is at heart a series of love poems. In the first selection, the maiden hears her beloved beckon her to leave with him into the new creations of springtime. In the second sequence, she implores his faithfulness, as the book reiterates the importance of love.

Tobit 8:5b–8, by contrast, depicts "older" love. The book comes from the Apocrypha, a collection of works generally dated after our Old Testament works but prior to the New Testament. Tobit conveys the point that God will be faithful to those who are faithful to him. The central figure, Tobias, is a widower, and Sarah had seen woe; but on their wedding night they pray to the God who had blessed them both and joined them together.

Psalms

Including one or more psalms is an option which parallels the eucharistic practice. A hymn or anthem may be used instead. The Prayer Book suggests these three psalms:

Psalm 67 (BCP 675) sings praise to God while asking God's blessing, that his ways may be known through all the earth.

Psalm 127 (BCP 782–783) looks to God as the one who builds a house and blesses a family.

Psalm 128 (BCP 783), along similar lines, expresses the idea that those who "fear the Lord and who follow in his ways" will prosper in family life.

Lections from the Epistles

Generically, the epistles are letters to early Christian churches. They often seek to articulate the nature of Christianity, while trying to explain how to live as a Christian. Marriage is one element of that life in response to God:

1 Corinthians 13:1–13 is Paul's famous chapter on the nature and pre-eminence of love—*agapé*, to transliterate the Greek term ("charity" in the King James Version). In advising the Christian community on how to relate to each other, Paul's words have general application, but they relate powerfully to marriage in particular.

Ephesians 3:14–19 envisions Christ's work in unifying all things in God. It prays for strength and love and the presence of Christ who brings these both; for understanding the cosmic measure of his love; and for "the fullness of God" which is the final result.

Ephesians 5:1–2, 21–33 likewise applies a commitment to Christ to everyday living, specifically within the family. While controversial to some because of apparent inequality between partners ("wives, be subject to your husbands," v. 22), the passage asks sacrificial love of husbands ("love your wives, just as Christ loved the church and gave himself up for her," v. 25) as they "love...their own bodies" (v. 28). The topic sentence of the key paragraph underscores being "subject to one another out of reverence for Christ" (v. 21).

Colossians 3:12–17 gives practical advice on how to live as followers of Christ in relationship with each other, citing qualities which should prevail among all—especially within the family.

1 John 4:7–16 connects the love of each other with the love of God as an expression in our world of the heavenly love God has first shown us in Christ.

Lections from the Gospels

By ancient custom, the congregation stands for the reading of the Gospel. As the story and words of Jesus, it has unique importance. For that reason, too, a member of the clergy reads this lesson; and it is preceded and followed by special announcement.

The Gospel lections, like those for the Epistle, place marriage within the wider context of responding to God. They each quote Jesus explaining to his disciples how to live:

Matthew 5:1–10 comprises the "Beatitudes," the first portion of the Sermon on the Mount. They set forth the way of the Christian in contrast to the way of the world.

Matthew 5:13–16 continues the "sermon" by posing now-familiar images. To be "salt of the earth" or "light of the world" looks beyond oneself to the role that the Christian—and the Christian marriage—plays in seasoning and enlightening the world beyond.

Matthew 7:21, 24–29 concludes this "sermon" with an admonition to act rather than simply to speak, and to establish one's life on a firm foundation—which, we can deduce, a marriage also needs.

Mark 10:6–9, 13–16 constitutes the clearest teaching ascribed to Jesus on marriage and family life, both regarding marriage and the place of children.

John 15:9–12 derives from the instructions of Jesus to his disciples at the Last Supper. He concentrates here on the unity which he strives to bring, and the importance of love in bringing about that unity among all his followers. He cites his own example as the model of how his followers should treat each other.

In asking couples to select passages for their wedding, I encourage them to look over all of them, for together these passages give insight into the biblical understanding of love, its relationship to God, especially through Jesus Christ, its practice and importance, and its role in the larger work of the Almighty.

Then this rubric appears on page 426 of the Prayer Book:

A homily or other response to the Readings may follow.

Responses could be nearly anything: music or song, full-length sermon (not desired by most couples!), a poem, conceivably even a liturgical dance. Though imagination can let loose, it must not run riot. Readings, often popular ones, pose a particular danger. Just because it sounds good or relates to relationships does not mean that it expresses a biblical notion of matrimony. Some have been known to contradict what the scriptural lessons have just declared. Instead, this is above all a response to the readings from the Bible. It follows the scriptural lessons and immediately precedes the most solemn moment of the entire ceremony. Whatever form it may take, the response must be carefully considered so that it will heighten the expression of Christian matrimony.

The Ministry of the Word—readings and responses—leads directly into the marriage itself. In light of what we have heard, marriage springs from the profoundest will of God that, in the words of one of the lections, we should "love one another as [Jesus] has loved you" (John 15:12).

The Marriage

*A*ll eyes now fix on the bridal pair. There is intensity in the moment, as if the eyes of heaven have joined the other witnesses. The couple, the priest and key attendants may step closer to the altar, the site of the sacrament of praise and thanksgiving.[40] The months and increasingly frenetic weeks of preparation culminate here and now. Years of their lives seem to lead to this moment.

The Vows

The couple, first one, then the other, with quiet promptings from the priest, take each other's hands to speak their love and commitment:

The Man, facing the woman and taking her right hand in his, says

In the Name of God, I, N., take you, N., to be my wife, to
have and to hold from this day forward, for better for worse,
for richer for poorer, in sickness and in health, to love and to
cherish, until we are parted by death. This is my solemn vow.

Then they loose their hands, and the Woman, still facing the man, takes his right hand in hers, and says

In the Name of God, I, N., take you, N., to be my husband,
to have and to hold from this day forward, for better for
worse, for richer for poorer, in sickness and in health, to love
and to cherish, until we are parted by death. This is my
solemn vow.

They loose their hands.

In the Name of God...

The "Name of God" is the name above all other names. Yet, unlike Muslims, who call him Allah, Christians and Jews do not claim to know what that name is. Exodus records the incident on Mount Horeb when God, responding to an inquisitive Moses from the burning bush, identifies himself elusively as "I AM" (Exodus 3:14). In biblical thought, knowing a person's name conveys his identity;

but God is so shrouded in transcendent mystery that he stands beyond and above our ability even to comprehend what he calls himself. (Similarly, God's mystery transcends the misleading gender-related pronouns we sometimes use to refer to "him.")

In the Bible, the phrase "the name of God" virtually means "God." When Abraham "called on the name of the Lord," he summoned the Almighty (e.g., Genesis 21:33, 26:25). When Moses banned the people from wrongly calling on God's name (one of the Ten Commandments, Exodus 20:7; Deuteronomy 5:11) or profaning it (e.g., Leviticus 18:21, 19:12, 21:6), he indicated that using the divine name is really the same as invoking the divinity. Knowing the name of the Lord—however ambiguous it might be—inspires reverence, awe, or even fear (Isaiah 52:6; Malachi 1:11–14), for it means knowing God in all the glory of the Almighty—even as God stands beyond knowing.

God stands as the ultimate authority. Even more, by his power, through his working and—as we will pray—by his blessing do man and woman come together as husband and wife. They enter their life together invoking the name of God.

...I, N., take you, N.,...

Now the couple identify each other. Names serve that purpose. At baptism the parents or sponsors, then the officiant, name the candidate at the very point of new life in Christ (BCP 307). The groom and, then in turn, the bride name themselves, then name the other, specifically, as if there were none other in the world, at the moment of this new creation in Christ. Generic love remains abstract; it is never real. Genuine fidelity or true love addresses itself specifically, one particular individual to another. "I, [fill in your name], take you [fill in his/her name]."

...to be my wife/husband...

For all these months and even years, the couple had grown closer and closer, so intimately close that they could think each other's thoughts, finish each other's sentences. They may have felt already married. Perhaps they moved in with each other as if they were virtually husband and wife, a practice now gaining in popularity even as sociologists challenge its long-range wisdom.[41] In terms we have been using, cohabitation involves a bond without a covenant.

Whatever the couple's state to this point, they were not married.

Now they commit. Formally. Unreservedly. Publicly. Unmistakably. Irrevocably. Completely—for now the process is truly complete. Now their married life begins.

...to have and to hold from this day forward...

The rubric instructs, "The Man, facing the woman and taking her right hand in his"; he holds her. Then, she takes his hand in hers; she holds him.

They hold each other. At their first dance in an hour or two, they will hold each other. That night, making love, they will hold each other as they will do so often on nights or mornings to come. When his father dies, when she loses her job, they hold each other. When their child is born, he holds her hand. And amazingly soon thereafter, when that child marries, they hold each other's hands once more.

The holding transcends the physical. Hardly an hour goes by without one having the other in mind. A business trip sends one across an ocean, but distance evokes an even deeper remembrance of the other. They argue one morning, and one of them storms off to the office, but work is futile, for thoughts of business cannot compete with thoughts of the other. John Winthrop, the seventeenth-century Puritan, and his wife Margaret agreed to think of each other every Monday and Friday between five and six o'clock while he sailed off from England to settle Boston.[42] Nowadays, air mail and E-mail, telephone, and fax make more direct, more frequent communication feasible. Modern means of "holding" help to ease physical separation.

...for better for worse, for richer for poorer, in sickness and in health...

The Prayer Book never sentimentalizes the world in which we live. It is a world of countless pleasures and multitudinous causes of bliss; but it also generates its troubles and griefs. Even the best of marriages cannot preclude the woes and evils that life inexorably begets, nor will it guarantee the good. But that is not the issue. Rather, the couple pledge to face all that this world presents them, together. They choose to become one, all in the name of God.

This is a love which recognizes the realities of life and transcends them. C. S. Lewis observed, "For this is one of the miracles of love;

it gives—to both, but perhaps especially to the woman—a power of seeing through its own enchantments and yet not being disenchanted."[43] We can hope that the man will do the same.

...to love and to cherish...

The vows are redefining our understanding of love well beyond hearts and flowers to the earnest, bold, and vibrant relationship of living in this world as husband and wife. Yet hearts and flowers remain a part of this love, as the term "cherish" connotes. Derived from the Latin *carus* (which also yields our term "charity," the word the King James Version of the Bible uses in that most popular of wedding readings, 1 Corinthians 13), the word "cherish" implies placing a high value, holding dear, appreciating, or—to use another derivation of *carus*—caressing. Amidst the sober realities of life, which marriage faces, comes also a tenderness within which the couple value and nurture each other. This is a relationship which does not ignore the stresses of a hard day at work but which, in the evening, soothes and restores. It is a relationship in which the couple care enough to deal with the strains and disagreements of living together while also treasuring and esteeming each other and, in the process, making all things well.

...until we are parted by death.

That's right, death ... and nothing less. Anything less than a lifetime commitment stands short of a total pledge. This is a faithfulness which matches that of Christ who was faithful unto his death.

But is that all? Just death? What about hereafter? Mormonism attracts some with the promise of being "married through eternity." But the concept of relationship beyond the grave abides in orthodox Christian experience. A parishioner was describing her journey of faith; when she spoke of her husband, who had died some years previously, she described their relationship in an offhanded but heartfelt way as "a marriage that sustains me still." Understanding the doctrine of the "communion of saints" reveals a sense of unity abiding among all Christians, past and present and even future, especially with those whom we particularly love. In dying and rising, Jesus opened a new dimension of life beyond the mortal. Those who "rest in Jesus" live on.[44] If Christian marriage is rooted in the experience of the Lord's resurrection, then it must, of course, transcend the grave, and can sustain us still.

This is my solemn vow.

He, then she, has said it—what was missing before, what made their relationship, no matter how strong, still incomplete: the commitment, solemnly spoken before the eyes of God and of the whole world (as represented by the few or many who, perhaps through tears, look on).* They are truly the ministers of this sacrament.

Sadly, not everyone who speaks these vows will abide by them. No, that is incorrect. No one who speak these vows will abide by them, not completely, not as they should. Loving and cherishing are too demanding for one hundred per cent compliance. Nonetheless, we speak the ideal. We promise to try, as hard as we possibly can, to give the very best we can to this person who promises to do the same. That is the nature of this cherishing love, this *agapé* which Paul described in 1 Corinthians 13. When—not if—we fail, we trust in God and in the person to whom we have given our vow to forgive. And we ask for help from God and from others, which, surely, is why nearly the next thing we do in the ceremony is to pray.

Having said that, we must add that, for some, abiding by their vows becomes impossible, and their marriages end in divorce. Many more fail to approximate the ideals with which they began. But the ideals remain valid nonetheless; and the hope always remains that, with help from God and others, the ideals will take hold anew.

Early in my ministry, a family in the parish who seemed so strong suddenly exploded. The divorce devastated their teenaged children, and, apparently, being separated became too much for them, too. In due course, they reunited, even stronger for having faced the gates of Hell. "This is my solemn vow."

---

*These are the groom's and bride's vows, and I strive mightily for them—not me—to speak them clearly and boldly. To assure this, I ask them to all but memorize their vows, so that they become more comfortable with what they will say and, even more important, truly understand what they will say. I want them to know what they are pledging; these are the vows that, hereafter, they will live by. When the time comes to say their vows, a few feel secure enough to recite them from memory (with me there to jog any memory); but most wish for me to phrase them out. I do so in the quietest possible voice, asking the couple to boom out so that what the congregation hears is each of them and not the priest: These are their vows.

The Blessing and Giving of Rings

The Priest may ask God's blessing on a ring or rings as follows

Bless, O Lord, *this ring* to be *a sign* of the vows by which
this man and this woman have bound themselves to each
other; through Jesus Christ our Lord. *Amen.*

*The giver places the ring on the ring-finger of the other's hand and
says*

N., I give you this ring as a symbol of my vow, and with all
that I am, and all that I have, I honor you, in the Name of
the Father, and of the Son, and of the Holy Spirit (*or* in the
Name of God).

Customs, once established, have the habit of abiding over
millennia. The wedding ring is a case in point. Using a ring to
symbolize marriage goes back at least to Romans of the first century.
Since a ring lacks beginning or end, a groom would give a ring to his
bride at their betrothal to symbolize fidelity. When the custom first
began, the ring was of iron. Later, the ring was made of finer metals,
especially gold; and both bride and groom would exchange rings.[45]

Converts to Christianity often brought older family practices with
them to church. The ring was one, and the Church appropriated the
symbol and in its marriage rites developed sometimes elaborate
ceremonies around the ring, its blessing, and its placement on the
finger. In medieval England, for instance, as the groom recited the
Trinitarian formula, he placed the ring on the bride's thumb when
mentioning the Father, on the index finger when citing the Son, on the
next finger when speaking of the Spirit, and, at the "Amen," onto the
"ring finger." There it remained, for it was believed (erroneously)
that a vein ran from that finger to the heart.[46] But woe to whomever
dropped it!—for, in time, that was deemed a bad omen for the
marriage.[47]

By the sixteenth century, the innocent little ring had become an
item of what now seems astonishing controversy. Puritans despised
it as one of three "noxious ceremonies" (common practices in the
church of their day that were not certified, Puritans believed, by
scriptural warrant).[48] Elizabethan Anglicans retorted by trotting out

quotations from early Christian writers that referred to even more ancient—if pagan—customs which the Church had begun to use for Godly purpose. As Richard Hooker argued for the Anglicans, the ring had served throughout Christian history "as a token of our purposed endless continuance in that which we never ought to revoke."[49]

Such disputes are long forgotten. Nowadays, brides and (almost always) grooms choose to give and wear this age-old symbol of faithfulness. Little do they realize that they follow the example of pre-Christian Romans.

The ring can become part of his or her very identity. A couple of years after my mother died, my father suffered a major stroke. For more than a week, he was virtually unaware of what was going on around him. At last, he began to "come to." One of the first signs of his return was an extreme discomfort on his left hand. It wasn't pain, for he had lost all feeling in it. But something was wrong. Something was missing. Hospital personnel had removed his wedding band. After nearly fifty years of wearing it ceaselessly, he missed it sorely. Mere death had not parted my mother from him. The symbol still held a mysterious power.

The groom or the couple or their attendants present the ring(s) or "bands" as some call them, a term which shares an Anglo-Saxon heritage with other pertinent words, like "bond" and "bind." The wedding "band" symbolizes the wedding "bond" as it "binds" the finger—and ideally the marriage—in an endless circle of faithfulness. Whatever the rings are called, old Prayer Book custom establishes that the rings are to be laid on the priest's book.[50] The priest then invokes God's blessing upon the ring(s) to be sign(s) of the couple's vows which bind them together.

English grooms until recently would place the ring on the bride's finger saying this: "With this ring I thee wed: with my body I thee worship: and with all my worldly goods I thee endow. In the name of the Father, and of the Son, and of the Holy Ghost. Amen."[51] Americans (in the 1928 Prayer Book) made the point more simply, "With this Ring I thee wed: In the Name of the Father, and of the Son, and of the Holy Ghost. Amen."[52] What couples now say underscores the ring, first, as symbol and, second, as a mark of total commitment in personal being ("with all that I am") and personal resources of every sort ("and all that I have").* The current Prayer Book recognizes that most couples now choose a double-ring ceremony, and yet the rubrics allow other suitable practices as well. Note, for example, the alternate wording in the blessing of the rings that allows a couple to be wed "in the Name of God" rather than "in the Name of the Father, and of the Son, and of the Holy Spirit"; also note "Additional Directions" rubrics (BCP 437) that permit a couple to dispense with rings entirely and choose "some other suitable symbol of the vows."

The Pronouncement

Then the Celebrant joins the right hands of husband and wife and says

Now that *N.* and *N.* have given themselves to each other by solemn vows, with the joining of hands and the giving and receiving of *a ring*, I pronounce that they are husband and wife, in the Name of the Father, and of the Son, and of the Holy Spirit.

Those whom God has joined together let no one put asunder.

People Amen.

Notice two elements: first, a rubric directing the priest to join their hands. Only moments earlier, the groom and then the bride each took the other's hand while speaking the vows, then loosed them—as instructed by the Prayer Book (BCP 427). Now the priest joins their hands together again for the next act of this drama, the exchange of rings. Second, notice the careful phrasing; naming each of the couple once more, the celebrant announces that they "have given themselves to each other" and have done so by their "solemn vows" and "the joining of hands," denoted by the giving and receiving of a ring or rings. That's it. Exact, yet so supremely spare and simple. Weddings can become productions worthy of Broadway; but no

---

*Among the topics a couple should discuss extensively are such matters as finances, salaries, bank accounts, budgets, spending, and saving. Though a formal "prenuptial agreement" may not be necessary, some clear, mutual understandings about money before the wedding day will ease life after it.

matter how many attend, or how numerous the bridesmaids, whether in the largest cathedral or the humblest chapel, at the heart of the marriage stand the bride and groom who marry each other in the quietness of vows, gifts, and joining hands. Nothing could be simpler, nor more profound. And such, so often, are the ways of God.

Note, too, that they marry *each other*. The officiant solemnizes, but they—husband and wife—are the ministers of this sacrament. They say their vows (no matter how much the officiant prompts them) and join hands; they will be the ones who consummate the marriage that night,[53] and begin living it out the next day or, more precisely, the next moment. Only within the last few hundred years has a priest been deemed necessary.[54] But the celebrant does officially represent Christ and his Church to oversee, lead, and (a bit later in the ceremony) to bless. Because of the blessing, a priest or bishop normally officiates, as they are the ones ordained by the Church with this responsibility. Still, the couple marry each other.

They do so, nonetheless, within the context of the Church. As a sign of that, the priest might wrap his stole* around the joined hands of the couple, an action that gave birth to the phrase, "tying the knot." It connotes both the sacramental unity of marriage and the fact that it occurs within the community of faith.[55]

Having done so, then the priest proclaims them as husband and wife to the assembled multitude and, truly, to the world.

He adds the final statement: "Those whom God has joined together let no one put asunder." The declaration derives from Jesus himself, who teaches the sanctity and permanence of marriage.[56] It also pronounces this marriage an act of God. Here at last is the revelation—so often hinted at but now made explicit at this culminating point of the ceremony—that it is God who unites these two as husband and wife. They have at the source of their relationship the creator and redeemer of all the world. And Jesus, ultimately, is the true minister of the sacrament.

They are married, now, in the eyes of God and all his cosmos.

---

*This vestment, usually white for weddings, is the long narrow scarf which hangs from the priest's neck, a symbol of sacramental authority within the Church.

The Prayers

Short of finding their wedding interrupted by the return in glory of our Lord Jesus, the bride and groom will soon emerge as a married couple who stand a good chance of enjoying at least some earthly time together. So, beginning with page 428 of the Prayer Book, we offer prayers for them which culminate with God's blessing.

The Lord's Prayer

All standing, the Celebrant says

Let us pray together in the words our Savior taught us.

People and Celebrant

Our Father, who art in heaven,
    hallowed be thy Name,
    thy kingdom come,
    thy will be done,
        on earth as it is in heaven.
Give us this day our daily bread.
And forgive us our trespasses,
    as we forgive those
        who trespass against us.
And lead us not into temptation,
    but deliver us from evil.
For thine is the kingdom,
    and the power, and the glory,
    for ever and ever. Amen.
	Our Father in heaven,
	    hallowed be your Name,
	    your kingdom come,
	    your will be done,
	        on earth as in heaven.
	Give us today our daily bread.
	Forgive us our sins
	    as we forgive those
	        who sin against us.
	Save us from the time of trial,
	    and deliver us from evil.
	For the kingdom, the power,
	    and the glory are yours,
	    now and for ever. Amen.

Consistently in the services of the Church, the prayer which Jesus taught immediately follows the key act or statement of that occasion: right after the prayer of consecration at Eucharist; right after the baptism (unless the baptism occurs within the Eucharist); and here, right after proclaiming God's act in uniting man and woman as husband and wife. Christ's words initiate a sequence of prayers for the two of them and for the world which Christ seeks to redeem. (To avoid duplication, the Lord's Prayer may be omitted here if it will be said later at the Eucharist.)

The Intercessions

The Deacon or other person appointed reads the following prayers, to which the People respond, saying, Amen.

If there is not to be a Communion, one or more of the prayers may be omitted.

Let us pray.

Eternal God, creator and preserver of all life, author of salvation, and giver of all grace: Look with favor upon the world you have made, and for which your Son gave his life, and especially upon this man and this woman whom you make one flesh in Holy Matrimony. *Amen.*

Give them wisdom and devotion in the ordering of their common life, that each may be to the other a strength in need, a counselor in perplexity, a comfort in sorrow, and a companion in joy. *Amen.*

Grant that their wills may be so knit together in your will, and their spirits in your Spirit, that they may grow in love and peace with you and one another all the days of their life. *Amen.*

Give them grace, when they hurt each other, to recognize and acknowledge their fault, and to seek each other's forgiveness and yours. *Amen.*

Make their life together a sign of Christ's love to this sinful and broken world, that unity may overcome estrangement, forgiveness heal guilt, and joy conquer despair. *Amen.*

Bestow on them, if it is your will, the gift and heritage of children, and the grace to bring them up to know you, to love you, and to serve you. *Amen.*

Give them such fulfillment of their mutual affection that they may reach out in love and concern for others. *Amen.*

Grant that all married persons who have witnessed these vows may find their lives strengthened and their loyalties confirmed. *Amen.*

Grant that the bonds of our common humanity, by which all your children are united one to another, and the living to the dead, may be so transformed by your grace, that your will may be done on earth as it is in heaven; where, O Father, with your Son and the Holy Spirit, you live and reign in perfect unity, now and for ever. *Amen.*

Now bride and groom can relax a bit. They have made it successfully through their lines. They have been declared wed. Their minds may wander.

In considering the prayers offered in the service, let us allow our minds to wander, too:

Imagine settling into a movie theater of gigantic dimensions, like the IMAX cinema at the Smithsonian Air and Space Museum in Washington. On this five-stories-tall screen, as prayers are being read, seem to appear images of the entire cosmic order. All creation flashes before us. So does God (not that God can be confined to anything, much less to a theater screen).

With this vast scope, the prayers begin:

Eternal God, creator and preserver of all life, author of salvation, and giver of all grace: Look with favor upon the world you have made, and for which your Son gave his life...

This is truly "big picture." The universe flashes before our eyes and, with it, the Lord who came to redeem what the Father created.

Suddenly the camera zooms in on two people:

...and especially upon this man and this woman whom you make one flesh in Holy Matrimony.

There they are, bride and groom, standing at the very center of creation, as if for this moment the eyes of the cosmos are upon them, freshly joined together by God. We hold them in focus for a time:

Give them wisdom and devotion in the ordering of their common life, that each may be to the other a strength in need, a counselor in perplexity, a comfort in sorrow, and a companion in joy.

Echoes of earlier themes return: In the bond of unity, the two of them can create a stronger entity than each operating alone. One can draw strength from the other, one can offer advice and insight to the other precisely because of their distinctiveness from each other.

Because they are one, they can "have and hold" each other through the crises and sorrows they face. They can rejoice together in the marvelous times that shall also come. They can even start at that very moment, as one grasps the hand of the other during the prayers.

When I was in seminary, I heard about a graduate school couple whose child was missing. The chaplain organized parties of students to help search for the boy. Along the way, he observed of this couple what is so often true, that when he weakens, she finds strength to go on; and when she falters, he is there: "a strength in need...a comfort in sorrow." As I recall, the child was found. If so, at that point, the couple truly became "companions of joy." Countless times since, in good times and bad, I have seen the truth of the chaplain's comments about couples.

Grant that their wills may be so knit together in your will, and their spirits in your Spirit, that they may grow in love and peace with you and one another all the days of their life.

In growing to love each other, we grow to love God. Jesus taught as much. Citing love of God and love of neighbor as the two great commandments, he called the second "like" the first (Matthew 22:37–40). But of course. If husband and wife deepen their love for each other in ways that extend those qualities we identified as characteristics of Christ himself, then they will "knit" themselves not only with each other but also with the Lord.

Marriage, then, is a dynamic process, always changing, ideally always progressing. As a couple's wills are "knit together" in God's will, they grow with each other, while also growing in God. In that light, Christ is the teacher. He, the perfect Bridegroom, sets the model while also providing the Spirit that helps each to become more and more like the model he sets. Through marriage, God can work to "conform" mortals to himself which, as Paul indicates,[57] is part of his entire purpose. In short, marriage can help us to become increasingly like Jesus, it furthers the process of conversion of souls, and it aids in the divine plan for the universe—and for us.

The focus of our camera has now widened. Where once only the wife and husband stood revealed, now the circle includes God. There it remains for another moment:

Give them grace, when they hurt each other, to recognize and acknowledge their fault, and to seek each other's forgiveness and yours.

"Love means not ever having to say you're sorry," goes a phrase from a once-popular novel and movie.[58] No way! Love means *having* to say you're sorry, every time you should. What's more, love *allows* saying you're sorry, knowing that forgiveness and reconciliation await. It takes courage to admit one's wrongs; but strength is something we ask God to give to the couple.

Marriage may be heavenly, but it still abides on frail earth among fallible people. Plus, it becomes more and more heavenly only through practice; and practice means making mistakes. "I'm sorry" become essential words to pack along the journey, for they will often be needed; and when used, they make the going easier by freeing the couple of burdens they need not carry.

As long as they are properly disposed of. That means, first, looking at what truly are the wrongs. A woman complained that her husband said to her, "I'm sorry I hurt your feelings," leaving him unrepentant of what he did to hurt her feelings in the first place.[59] Second, forgiveness entails truly apologizing: regretting one's fault, admitting to it, and striving both to rectify the wrong and to see that it does not happen again (what is termed "amendment of life"). Furthermore, asking forgiveness means facing one's spouse but God, too, in order to attain full reconciliation; also, it means opening anew to the strength and grace which comes from "above" as well as from the person lying on the adjacent pillow. Finally, forgiveness must be offered by the one offended and accepted by the offender: "Forgive us our sins, as we forgive those who sin against us."

Forgiving each other in matrimony, then, teaches another lesson of heaven.

Make their life together a sign of Christ's love to this sinful and broken world, that unity may overcome estrangement, forgiveness heal guilt, and joy conquer despair:

The Exhortation introduced the theme of "sign"(recall the association of "sign" and "sacrament"). Now, the prayer recalls that great ideal, as our circle of focus widens to embrace the world about the couple.

Marriage is an "outward and visible sign," not a private one. Neither is it static. If husband and wife are happy and joyous, embodying to any degree those qualities of our Lord that we identified, then some of that joy or patience or trust is bound to spill out. So let it! When a couple allows others to see the reality of God's presence abiding in them, the two become a "light of the world" as Jesus foretold (Matthew 5:14); and the world becomes a better place.

Bestow on them, if it is your will, the gift and heritage of children, and the grace to bring them up to know you, to love you, and to serve you:[*]

Again the focus expands, this time to encompass the children who may arrive in due course. (Despite eager wishes of potential grandparents, the prayer suggests no time frame for their arrival.) Recalling for us one purpose of marriage—"the procreation and nurture of children in the knowledge and love of the Lord"— the prayer asks both for the "gift and heritage of children" and the blessing needed to rear them to know, love, and serve God.

Any "light" beaming forth from a marriage will radiate first on its children. They can grow by it to understand the nature of love and of God. In so doing the parents even become "evangelists"—sharers of the good news of God in Christ—teaching their children not just by what they say but by how they live. In that unique setting, they "represent Christ and his Church." The family, defined and ordered by the light of God, becomes one vitally significant setting in which the love of the resurrected Lord takes on an abiding reality. Thereby, too, the nuclear family becomes a model for forgiveness and reconciling love.

As the family never exists in isolation, there is still more:

---

[*]*This prayer is marked as optional, and it should be omitted in some cases. To include it at a wedding of two septuagenarians would seem odd to say the least. Other circumstances may suggest alteration of the prayer, rather than omission. The prayer of bestowal of children might be adapted, for example, to recognize existing children of the bride or groom. Consult "An Order for Marriage (BCP 435–436) for rubrics governing such alterations.*

Give them such fulfillment of their mutual affection that they may reach out in love and concern for others:

Our focus increases still more to include those around the couple, whether they be in need or in joy: parents and grandparents, children and grandchildren, friends and coworkers, neighbors, community, church. A strong and healthy marriage primarily benefits the couple itself and any children who come along. Yet, it profoundly, if subtly, influences those beyond the home. For if husband and wife are happy, joyous, and compassionate toward each other, they will not be able to keep those attributes to themselves. On the contrary, they will naturally extend those qualities to others around them. Holy Matrimony can bring to others the joys of heaven through the husband and wife who themselves savor what God has to offer.

Grant that all married persons who have witnessed these vows may find their lives strengthened and their loyalties confirmed:

Reaching out can start right now. Our "camera" now includes in the picture many present at the ceremony itself.

Think of the last wedding you attended. What did you contemplate? If you were then engaged or heading in that direction, you may have thought of your own upcoming wedding: How many attendants do I want? What will the flowers look like? What might the groomsmen wear? Why did they play *that*? In short, along with due appreciation for the bride and groom, you concentrate on the *wedding*.

Those who are married tell me that they think more of marriage, especially *their* marriage. They recall a spat earlier that week, gracefully mended; they remember their own ceremony, years before, and the ups and downs ever since (with the "ups" prevailing). While watching this new couple saying their vows, witnesses in the congregation reach over to grasp spouses' hands in gestures of love and cherishing, even now, all these years later.

After one wedding which I solemnized, the groom's father described troubles he and his wife had been facing so severe as to cause thoughts of divorce. But, he added, simply watching his son marry his new daughter-in-law gave him new commitment to his own marriage. Through his son's marriage, he and his wife found "their lives strengthened and their loyalties confirmed."

God's grace may abound from marriage in the simplest ways, even just by getting married.

Grant that the bonds of our common humanity, by which all your children are united one to another, and the living to the dead, may be so transformed by your grace, that your will may be done on earth as it is in heaven...

Again we return to the "big screen." The scene of cosmic proportions returns. One difference, though: we have placed the groom and bride within the larger context of humanity and also of God's redeeming purpose and plan. For they have a role to play. The world will not rise or fall on them alone. Let's not overstate the case, but let's not understate it either. What they do as husband and wife, and how they fulfill the ideals which the Church and they hold for themselves, influences the rest of society.

Much is made of the divorce rate. Splitting up devastates the couple and the children; and it subtly undermines the well-being of society. If bad marriages affect our world negatively, then it follows that good marriages provide a positive influence. By being happy, by developing a strong sense of family, by expressing love for each other not only in word but in hourly thought and in daily deed, by "reach[ing] out in love and concern for others," a husband and wife share in the reform of their world. This, too, is "ministry," a form of serving God.

They do more. They help to transform it into what God intends for all. In responding to what they perceive to be a call of God, they place themselves under his grace and ever-so-gentle rule. In bringing unity out of division, they both manifest and advance that divine purpose of bringing all things into one under the lordship of Christ. In the daily routine of their lives, as they show forth those qualities of Jesus toward each other and toward those about them, they grow in Christ themselves, which always is a basic goal of the Christian life. They also allow him to be known by others as they share his love in the world. Unconsciously, husband and wife become that "salt of the earth" and the "light of the world" that Jesus describes in Matthew 5:13–16, a passage that is one of the suggested readings for the marriage rite (BCP 426). Through their joy and peace and unity, they allow God to continue the process of transforming the world, reconciling it to himself and bringing all things into one under his most gracious will, "on earth as it is in heaven."

The Blessing of the Marriage

*A*fter all of that, what the couple most need is God's grace to pursue all they have begun.

Historically, the blessing of the marriage constituted one of the two great elements of the rite, the other being the consent of the couple as asked by the officiant on behalf of the Church (and state) and as spoken in their vows.[60] From these two basics, we may deduce two deep realities of matrimony. On the one hand, it is acutely personal, arising from the deepest desires of two people to come together in love to create a new family. On the other hand, marriage is mysteriously divine, arising from a basic will and purpose of God for these persons and for the world he created. Each of these realities is of serious consequence to Christians. As a result, the Church bears an enormous concern both for the individuals who are part of it, and for the Lord's greater designs which transcend it.

By his command, and with his authority, the Church bestows God's blessing upon the couple. In witness to this awesome grandeur, the couple kneel. They (and we) prepare for that blessing by one final prayer, for which the Prayer Book offers two choices. We will consider each in turn.

Most gracious God, we give you thanks for your tender love in sending Jesus Christ to come among us, to be born of a human mother, and to make the way of the cross to be the way of life. We thank you, also, for consecrating the union of man and woman in his Name. By the power of your Holy Spirit, pour out the abundance of your blessing upon this man and this woman. Defend them from every enemy. Lead them into all peace. Let their love for each other be a seal upon their hearts, a mantle about their shoulders, and a crown upon their foreheads. Bless them in their work and in their companionship; in their sleeping and in their waking; in their joys and in their sorrows; in their life and in their death. Finally, in your mercy, bring them to that table where your saints feast for ever in your heavenly home; through Jesus Christ our Lord, who with you and the Holy Spirit lives and reigns, one God, for ever and ever. *Amen.*

New to the 1979 Prayer Book, this intercession combines themes of great theology and everyday existence, reiterating our point all along that theology and life closely interrelate. The first sentence starts with incarnation ("we give you thanks for your tender love in sending Jesus Christ to come among us, to be born of a human mother"), then moves to redemption and atonement that makes us "at one" with God in a way that, by its linguistic ambiguity, can refer to Jesus and/or to us ("to make the way of the cross to be the way of life"). The second sentence more specifically mentions God's "consecrating" Holy Matrimony. It leads to a third sentence which shifts the focus to the man and woman kneeling before the altar. These overarching realities of God's kingdom—incarnation, redemption, atonement, and the way of the cross—apply to *them*; Christmas and Good Friday affect their lives as intimately as marriage itself, leading to the risen life in God. Not only does that bring Easter into view, but also the day of Pentecost when the Spirit rushed upon the disciples and began transforming them; here the priest invokes the same Spirit to "pour out the abundance" of God's blessing upon the kneeling couple.

Subsequent imagery draws from both Bible and this very liturgy. The seal recalls the ring, the mantle hints at festal clothing worn for weddings, and the crown derives from Eastern rites, for during Orthodox weddings crowns are held over the bride and groom.[61] Finally, the reference to the "table" looks beyond the altar where they kneel (and may soon share in Eucharist)—not to mention the banquet table of the reception where they will feast—to the heavenly banquet "where saints feast forever." Marriage looks to this life, but also into the eternity of Christ's kingdom.

The Prayer Book provides a second option:

> O God, you have so consecrated the covenant of marriage
> that in it is represented the spiritual unity between Christ
> and his Church: Send therefore your blessing upon these your
> servants, that they may so love, honor, and cherish each other
> in faithfulness and patience, in wisdom and true godliness,
> that their home may be a haven of blessing and peace;
> through Jesus Christ our Lord, who lives and reigns with you
> and the Holy Spirit, one God, now and for ever. *Amen.*

This adapts in modern language a traditional prayer used in the 1928 Prayer Book, itself derived from a prayer used since 1549. It briefly recapitulates themes we have seen throughout the liturgy: the "spiritual unity between Christ and his Church"; the plea for blessing so that the couple may "love, honor, and cherish each other"; the nature of their relationship characterized by "faithfulness and patience" and "wisdom and true godliness," the end result of which is a "home [that] may be a haven of blessing and peace," sanctuary amidst the woes of this world, or, more positively, a veritable outpost of the kingdom of heaven.

With that introduction, then follows the blessing:

> God the Father, God the Son, God the Holy Spirit, bless,
> preserve, and keep you; the Lord mercifully with his favor
> look upon you, and fill you with all spiritual benediction and
> grace; that you may faithfully live together in this life, and
> in the age to come have life everlasting. *Amen.*

What we have seen, we believe deeply to be the will and purpose of God the Father who creates, God the Son who redeems, and God the Holy Spirit who sanctifies (makes holy). In the name of the fullness of the Godhead, the couple receive the Trinitarian blessing both for this life and the life to come, looking always to the blessings of now and also of eternity. And so God bestows his grace, in a moment of sacrament and in the life of love which now begins in earnest and in bliss.

And we pray, thereby, that they may discover the joys of the world to come in the here and now of their life together as husband and wife, blessed by God.

In witness to that love, the couple then stand and the celebrant declares,

	The peace of the Lord be always with you.
People	And also with you.

As a liturgical expression of the stereotypical "You may kiss the bride," which clergy used to say, these words prompt the couple to "greet each other," as the Prayer Book somewhat euphemistically phrases it. Members of the congregation also share gestures of fellowship and joy with each other and sometimes even with the couple who now have become one in the sight of them all. This exchange of greetings (known as "The Peace") is one last symbol of love and faithfulness and union before God and the company of witnesses before the couple head down the aisle as husband and wife.

What God has joined together, let no one put asunder.

Banquet

*H*istorically, weddings and feasts have gone together like brides and grooms. The feast may be small or large. I have attended everything from an early-morning breakfast at home for six humans plus two dogs, to a potluck affair in the parish hall, to a large-scale country club bash worthy of its Texas locale. No matter the size or scope or cost of the party, the joy, conviviality, and fellowship of sharing food and drink on this particularly happy day seems to exhilarate all those who are there.

The Church has its own sacramental banquet, the Eucharist. Perhaps as early as the sixth century, the Church invited its people to unite in Holy Matrimony in the context of this feast of the Lord. It became the standard setting for marriages in Roman Catholicism, and Anglican leaders during the Reformation expected it. Custom, though, soon evolved in a different direction, and for centuries the "nuptial Eucharist" became a rarity.[62]

The 1979 Book of Common Prayer revised the entire rite in such a way as to recommend it once more for those who wish it. By including "propers" (a collect, lessons, and psalms) along with intercessory prayers and the Peace, the basic structure of the marriage ceremony parallels the "Ministry of the Word" of the Eucharist. These features, together with the special proper preface and postcommunion prayer (BCP 349, 381, 432), make it easy to incorporate wedding and Eucharist. This single, if two-pronged, experience celebrates, as can no other act of the people of God, the presence of Christ and, indeed, the whole "company of heaven" in the ultimate act of Christian worship.

The Offertory

The instructions on page 432 of the Prayer Book say,

The liturgy continues with the Offertory, at which the newly married couple may present the offerings of bread and wine.

The "Offertory" is the moment when the people present their offerings to God. In American churches on Sundays that generally includes bringing forth the bread and wine to be used at the Eucharist along with the monetary gifts which the congregation places in basins or baskets. Despite temptations to fathers of brides or to clergy at big weddings, collection plates are not passed at weddings. But the altar must be prepared for the eucharistic banquet.

For the couple as their first joint action as husband and wife to present the elements which shall become the Body and Blood of Christ constitutes another statement of faith. "All things come of thee, O Lord," goes a familiar sentence, "and of thine own have we given thee."[63] The newly married return to God for his use what has come from him, just as the love which they share derives from the heavenly Father. Friends or family may carry the bread and wine instead.

While the holy table is prepared, music is often played or sung, following the practice of what happens in many churches on Sundays. This music might be a piece played by the organist or other instrumentalist(s), a work sung by soloist or choir, or a hymn in which the congregation can join. Again the selection of the music itself and who performs it must be made with care. Choices may range from joyously exuberant to quietly meditative; but like all the music in the nuptial service, it should express the themes of the celebration in a way that glorifies our God. Inviting a cousin whose voice sounds terrific coming from the shower to warble "O Promise Me" may win points on the sentimentality scale but ends up embarrassing everyone. Some couples, instead, accept the Prayer Book's suggestion of using a hymn here or elsewhere as a means of expressing joy or prayer or praise in a way that involves the whole congregation.[64]

The Preface

Prior to the "Sanctus"—"Holy, holy, holy Lord" (BCP 334, 362)—the celebrant says a "preface" which picks up and extends the tone of the celebration. The Preface for Marriage is as follows for both the traditional language of Rite I and the contemporary language of Rite II, respectively:

Because in the love of wife and husband, thou hast given us an image of the heavenly Jerusalem, adorned as a bride for her bridegroom, thy Son Jesus Christ our Lord; who loveth her and gave himself for her, that he might make the whole creation new. (BCP Rite I 349)

Because in the love of wife and husband, you have given us an image of the heavenly Jerusalem, adorned as a bride for her bridegroom, your Son Jesus Christ our Lord; who loves her and gave himself for her, that he might make the whole creation new. (BCP Rite II 381)

The preface reiterates a powerful theme from the last book of the Bible. Revelation 21:2 looks to the final victory of God; as John the Divine writes, "I saw the holy city, the new Jerusalem, coming down out of heaven from God, prepared as a bride adorned for her husband." Hebrews 12:22 also refers to the heavenly Jerusalem as "the city of the living God." Ephesians 5:25–27 speaks of the relationship between Christ and the Church as one of love comparable to marriage (recall our earlier examination of "The Exhortation"). Jesus alluded to bridegrooms in teaching of his kingdom, especially the parable in Matthew 25:1–13.[65] The preface recalls all these, while pointing toward the new and risen life of all creation (see 2 Corinthians 5:17).

The Communion

Again a rubrical suggestion:

At the Communion, it is appropriate that the newly married couple receive Communion first, after the ministers.

Now the husband and wife receive Communion. They join thereby in the heavenly banquet, together with "angels and archangels and all the company of heaven." Even more significantly, they join with their Lord in the communion of his body and blood. For the couple to "receive Communion first" implies that others, too, will join them in the next moments; the sacrament unites them thereby with those about them, and, indeed, the whole Church of Christ.

The Postcommunion Prayer

All being done, there remains but a prayer of thanksgiving and closing, which in a nuptial Eucharist rightly recognizes both the redemptive act of God in Jesus Christ and the more specific redemptive act in joining two people as husband and wife.

> O God, the giver of all that is true and lovely and gracious:
> We give you thanks for binding us together in these holy
> mysteries of the Body and Blood of your Son Jesus Christ.
> Grant that by your Holy Spirit, *N.* and *N.*, now joined in Holy
> Matrimony, may become one in heart and soul, live in fidelity
> and peace, and obtain those eternal joys prepared for all who
> love you; for the sake of Jesus Christ our Lord. *Amen.*

Dominating this prayer is the theme of God's unifying activity, which we know through Christ who utilizes Eucharist and matrimony to help attain his purpose. The prayer presents the themes of this unity, fidelity, and peace one final time, looking ahead (as does the nuptial blessing) to the end of the ages, all through Jesus Christ.

Whether or Not to Include the Eucharist

When Melissa and I were married back in the days of the "old" Book of Common Prayer (1928), we wanted to include the Eucharist (or "Holy Communion" as it was more commonly known then) as part of the service. It was not an easy fit, though we made it work. Communion in this context was a rarity for many of our guests, but, fortunately, they commended our decision.

The 1979 Prayer Book changed all that. It makes the rite of matrimony within the eucharistic celebration much more feasible. It also has made it more familiar. Still, even with the renewed emphasis, the idea of a "nuptial Eucharist" remains rather novel for many. Given the enormous centrality of Communion in our personal and corporate spiritual lives, however, this option deserves serious consideration.

What are some reasons why and why not?

Some say, **"It takes too long."** In my experience, it adds fifteen to thirty minutes to a ceremony. What is that within the months or years of preparation, or in light of the years to come?

"Logistics inhibit it." This is a consideration that is more likely to arise if the wedding is being held in a place other than a church building. Although Communion can be celebrated "in all times and in all places," it is easier to do so in some places, such as a church, than in others. The practicalities of a wedding outside of a church building pose one set of challenges; having Eucharist, as well, adds others. If, however, these difficulties can be resolved, the result can be a very moving experience. Talk with the priest about what is permissible, feasible, and recommended.

"It might offend some people in the congregation." So might the use of the term "God." Guests generally understand that they will attend a Christian wedding; if that offends them, they will not come. For Christians to meet in their own church to practice their faith, even in the presence of nonbelievers, is no shame. The scandal would be if we did anything else.

Probably not everyone in the congregation will actually receive Communion. Yet we need not presume that they abstain out of pique. Just as some, for their own reasons, will abstain from eating meat or wedding cake at the reception, so there are often wedding guests who, for whatever reasons, refrain from receiving Communion; they do not intend offense, and none should be taken.

"Only the bride and groom should receive communion." That strikes me as similar to permitting only the bride and groom to have wedding cake at the reception. Not all guests will wish to eat cake, but all who are part of the body of Christ should feel welcome to do so nonetheless. In light of the unifying nature of matrimony and Eucharist alike—and of the clear implication of the rubric stating that the couple will receive Communion "first" (BCP 432)—I strongly urge couples to invite all baptized members of the congregation who wish to receive to do so. Furthermore, as we have seen repeatedly, the congregation "represent[s] Christ and his Church" (BCP 855) and, therefore, should share in the eucharistic celebration of the community of faith gathered there.

"One family or one of the couple is not Episcopalian." This concern is especially legitimate, and it should be discussed carefully with the officiant. Both matrimony and the Eucharist aim to unify, not to exclude. If one of the couple or a large number of family and friends are bound by conscience or denominational dictum from receiving Holy Communion in an Episcopal church, then Communion may not be a good idea. This raises anew the deeper pastoral question of denominational ties and religious expectations of the partners. In their preparation, the couple should candidly explore with the priest what they intend for their lives of faith. As important as choosing a home in which to live is choosing a spiritual home in which to worship God and to grow with his people who gather there.

Holy Eucharist and Holy Matrimony share a vital characteristic. Both aim to attain "communion," a "union with." In one case, the union is most directly between man and woman. In the other, it is with God. As the fellowship of the wedding reception allows the joy of bride and groom to spread among those who participate, so the Eucharist aims at incorporating everyone who shares in it the more solemn but no less joyous presence of God and, specifically, of Jesus, our heavenly bridegroom. As we celebrate the joining together of man and woman, we also celebrate the union of God with humanity through Christ who is sacramentally present in his body and blood. Neither union is ultimately fulfilled on that day; but both offer the promise of ever-deepening unity—unity one with another and the unity of all God's faithful people with their Lord.

If Holy Eucharist is something which the couple wish to share with one another and with those who gather about them—and if it all makes good sense—then do it!

Postlude: Toward a More Perfect Wedding

At the outset, I foreswore inflicting another "how-to" wedding guide. This book has been about the nature of matrimony, not the logistics of bringing it about. However, because I have participated in nearly 300 weddings, certain principles have evolved in my mind. Far from being hard-and-fast "rules," what follow are "ideas." The authority on what to do is the parish priest who knows what works in the particular setting and has ideas of his or her own. Still, let me share some notions:

Principle #1: Meet early with the clergy.

Make an appointment soon after the engagement, for several vital reasons:

- Can the priest officiate? That is, do the couple meet the canonical requirements, is the priest willing to officiate, and do the priest's and the parish's calendars permit? Obviously, the sooner you make arrangements, the more choices and flexibility you have in case your first choice of date is not possible.

- You can begin meeting with your priest to begin the premarital discussions. For one thing, you can address logistical details. Far more importantly, you and the priest will have the opportunity of visiting with each other over a period of a time during which your relationship as a couple will be evolving. As you face joys and tensions together, you may find it highly useful to have an objective, experienced friend to help put these into perspective; and when you arrive at the altar, you will look up at a reassuring countenance you have come to know well.

- You can begin planning the ceremony in an increasingly thoughtful, educated way, and the result will be more meaningful, especially for the two of you and, therefore, for all.

One further observation: couples who set the date for the ceremony based on the logistics of the reception strike clergy as having reversed priorities. Call your priest *before* you call your caterer.

Principle #2: This is a service of the Church.

Intimately personal, a family celebration, Holy Matrimony is more still—a time when the people of God worship their Lord whom they see acting at that very moment. It is never private, even though the public need not be invited. On the other hand, a wedding is a corporate act, part of something larger, as, indeed, marriage entails far more than the two who marry. And Holy Matrimony is above all an act that occurs within that "community of faith" to which I have so often referred.

Every parish church and every priest has standard procedures usually emerging from practical experience and theological conviction. Find out what those standards may be and ask what leeway you might have for personal choice. As the wise priest allows some flexibility, so the wise couple respect the clergy's position. After all, the priest has probably been involved in more weddings than the couple or even the mother of the bride! (So-called "wedding directors" may not be necessary or desirable or even permitted. Before asking someone to assist, check with the priest.)

Principle #3: Start early on all your planning.

Whether you have three weeks or twelve months, the job will explode to fill the time you have—and then some. Get started as early as possible, not only with clergy but also with others. But you don't need to do it all at once either. Pace yourself. You'll have time to deal with the unexpected in a more relaxed way. Even so:

Principle #4: Something will go wrong.

Regardless of how early you start or how thorough the preparation, something will not go according to plan. You have no idea what it will be. Maybe the cake falls over, a bridesmaid trips, or the electricity pumping the organ suddenly goes out. As long as the two of you are married to each other in the eyes of God, and all are healthy, whatever goes wrong *does not matter*. What truly counts is what *does* happen—that you two become wife and husband.

In fact, whatever does go wrong may be what people remember most fondly. One couple decided to use a relative, who was an accomplished pianist but not a practiced church musician, as the organist. Experienced church organists know that bridal parties do not necessarily process in perfect keeping with the timing and duration of the music as it is written. As a concert musician, this person played the wedding march from start to grand finish ... and quit—even though the bride and her father were but halfway down the aisle. Five years later, when that bride's sister planned a ceremony, the family was still amused by the day the music died.

To help mitigate Principle #4, remember #5, #6, and #7:

Principle #5: Keep it simple.
Weddings can get out of hand, as every couple almost immediately discover. Along with social obligations (such as whom you should invite), and images of The Perfect Wedding done just the "right" way, come enormous tensions. Remember that the more you do, the more there is to go wrong, the more there is to worry about, and the more you have to pay. Ask if something is truly necessary or merely "nice." Even more, does it "fit" what you are striving to achieve?— and what might that be?

Principle #6: There are "traditions," and there is Tradition.
That is, not all that we classify as "traditional" is as important as people think. For instance:

- The bride does not have to wear white nor does the groom need to be dolled up in black tie. In medieval custom, the bride simply wore her finest dress regardless of the color, and no moral conclusions were drawn from her choice. The bride, the groom, and their attendants are free to wear what makes good sense.

- It is no more mandatory for the bride to process to "Here Comes the Bride" than it is for the couple to honeymoon at Niagara Falls. In fact, given that the tune comes from a German opera involving a pagan goddess, its use is questionable at best. It has also become a virtual cliché of weddings—especially when a rich diversity of wonderful music exists. Instead of copying what others do or relying on recordings of "wedding music," speak with your priest and the organist.

- It has become all too customary in various churches in the United States for wedding processions to go something like this: groomsmen (who may slip down a side aisle), bridesmaids, ringbearer, flower girl, and attendant of honor all enter first; so far so good. In this scenario, though, the congregation remains seated; then, all rise for the grand entrance of the bride who processes down the aisle alone, but for her escort. I find several problems with this last set of details: First, it can be painful and impractical for the congregation to remain seated while craning necks to see those who precede the bride; beyond that, it may be inappropriate for them to remain seated if the procession is headed by the cross or if a hymn is being sung.* More importantly, this tradition is a real departure from the Anglican heritage that created the Episcopal Church. In the Church of England, by contrast, the bride generally heads her procession, with attendants—usually younger girls, sometimes a few pageboys—following. No other ritual of the Episcopal Church lavishes this kind of attention on one person—neither on a candidate for baptism, nor on a candidate for ordination as deacon or priest, nor on a bishop-elect being consecrated bishop. In fact, if the Archbishop of Canterbury himself were paying the Episcopal Church a visit, not even he would presume to make such an entrance! I am not trying to deny the bride her moment of honor, but I am suggesting that we not allow ill-considered habits, especially those shaped more by secular culture, to turn the marriage rite into an ostentatious show. The art, I believe, is to find that fine line between good taste and affectation, between good sense and confusion, between an understanding of the wedding as a religious event, befitting the house of God and the community of God, and an understanding of it as an opportunity for prestige-enhancement and social display. To that end, Church tradition, the counsel of the officiating priest, the conventions of the parish, the practicalities of the ceremony and its setting, as well as the personal concerns of the bride and groom all should be considered with particular care. And ultimately, no matter what, all eyes will rightly be upon the bride.

---

*Note the music rubric which states that, "During their entrance, a hymn, psalm, or anthem may be sung" (BCP 423). Note also the discussion of Offertory music presented earlier (see "The Offertory"), much of which applies equally well to any nuptial music.

- Neither church law nor social necessity obligates spending hundreds on flowers and thousands on a reception. This is not a time when parents must repay social obligations. It is a celebration which can be as frugal or as fulsome as good sense and taste may dictate.

At heart, the elegant simplicity of the Episcopal service focuses with beaming clarity upon what truly does matter: the bride and groom, brought together in love by God and before God, joining themselves to each other in the name of God. All things should reflect, express or amplify this crystalline view. Anything which may distract should be avoided.

Photography is a common case in point. Matrimony is neither a "photo-op" nor an excuse for photographers to exhibit their artistry. Clicking buttons or grinding rewind motors can resound in the quiet of the church; and the flash of a camera from the congregation can momentarily blind the celebrant, I can tell you. If I have spots on my eyes, then I cannot see the book in front of me, the one with the couple's names clearly written; and—even though I know the service nearly by heart and have become close friends with the couple—in my panic my mind may go blank. And I really do want to get it right. So most parishes have clear guidelines about what photographers or videographers, professional or amateur, may and may not do. The couple should find out what the rules are and convey them to the photographer.* Responsible professionals always will cooperate, and their artistry still will manage to emerge.

Adding symbol to symbol is another possible distraction. The quiet drama of joining hands, exchanging rings, sealing all that happens with a kiss, and, in many weddings, joining in sacramental Communion with their Lord expresses in the simplest but clearest of ways the profoundest of truths about God's love for us, into which he calls us for each other. Though not all agree on the point,[66] further symbols may interfere with the clarity the rite now conveys. One

---

*And to the degree possible, to the congregation. For instance, if there is a bulletin or service sheet, a note may be added asking the congregation to refrain from taking pictures during the service; if there is an opportunity for picture-taking following the ceremony, this probably should be added to the note as well. As for professional photographers, some parishes communicate their rules and expectations to them directly.

such innovation, in my opinion, is the "unity candle." This is a gadget with three candles. The two mothers each light one prior to the service. After being pronounced husband and wife, each one takes the taper lighted earlier by their respective mothers and together light the larger, central candle, sometimes blowing out the candles they are holding before replacing them. Innovations such as the unity candle are not anticipated within the liturgy as it now stands; and they may create logistical difficulties, such as the time the bride got tangled in the train of her dress when trying to light the couple's candle. A colleague of mine once wondered, too, about what might be symbolized—unintentionally—by extinguishing the candles representing the mothers!

On the other hand, elements of family or ethnic tradition can sometimes deepen the meaning of the rite. Whether old or new, additions must never obscure the fundamental tradition of the Church regarding the nature and expression of Holy Wedlock. Any changes or substitutions (see the rubric allowing "some other suitable symbol...in place of the ring," BCP 437) should be considered judiciously in this light and thoughtfully explored with the priest.

Principle #7: Remember, you are entering Holy Matrimony.

An enormous emotional gap often divides "wedding" from "marriage": "wedding" is a day; "marriage" is a lifetime. Too easily can couples and their families become so distracted by the real or imagined necessities of the process of getting married that they overlook the greater dynamic of what is happening. May none of them lose focus on what the process is about and what man and woman and God are doing.

Here is one suggestion that I have passed along over the past twenty-five years to every couple whose marriage I have solemnized: sometime within the week prior to the rehearsal, the couple are to go out by themselves on a "date." It can be any setting or format you wish. Just one catch: neither may speak of the wedding, the reception, the dresses, the photographer, the cake, the music, or anything else pertaining to the process of getting married. Of marriage, they may talk for hours. Of the wedding? Not one minute!

Many of those couples have thanked me afterwards.

Principle #8: You are not alone. Ever.

We have explored marriage as a corporate event, a moment of great change, not merely for bride and groom, but also for their families, friends, society, and the community of faith. Joining in that community's life can become an enriching experience for the marriage, and for the community, too.

The banns have been a traditional way of announcing a forthcoming marriage. Prayers may be even more appropriate. A parish (in its Sunday and weekday intercessions) and individuals (in prayer groups and prayer chains) can anticipate or give thanks for the wedding in ways that undergird it with a spiritual power and allow those individuals, small groups, and the parish as a whole to join in the occasion, even if few actually attend.

But being part of a community of faith means most for a couple when they actually participate with that community. Perhaps you have recently moved to a new city and plan to be married in a church that is new to you. Attend Sunday services beforehand. Come to know its style, its clergy, its parishioners. Not only will you feel more comfortable on your wedding day, you will feel "at home" afterward.

The same principle applies if you are living in one place but plan to be married in another. For example, your wedding will be held where you grew up or went to college. In such a case, find a parish near where you will be living, a parish in which the two of you feel comfortable, and begin the process of belonging. It may not be your chosen wedding site, but it can still become your parish home.

In fact, you may find it convenient to meet for the premarital conversations with a priest in your new locality, though this should be discussed with the prospective officiant of your wedding. Let us say that a bride grew up in a town in Virginia and wants to be married there, but she and her fiancé live and work in Boston. It just makes sense for them to hold most of the premarital conversations with a priest in Boston, even though they will return to Virginia for their nuptials. The connection with the Boston priest, in turn, can foster for the couple what will become an ongoing relationship with the local New England parish; they will have found a new parish home for themselves. However, for this process to work, all concerned must be in agreement. In my experience, agreement is readily forthcoming, but, again, speak with your officiant.

Some get married in a familiar ecclesiastical haunt. Maybe you grew up in the parish where you will be wed, but you haven't worshiped there consistently. Perhaps you left for a time, during which the clergy and congregation changed; get to know it anew. Remember that you have changed also. Be aware that others in the parish would like the opportunity to get to know this "new" you— and also your spouse-to-be. It could be that your affianced is not familiar with your church or, perhaps, not familiar with any church. If so, this is a great time for your church and your beloved to come to know each other. Or perhaps, as another example, you both are already part of the congregation. Perhaps you even met one another while attending services here and you honestly do think of the congregation as your church "family." I have heard of such couples deciding to invite everybody in the parish to attend their wedding.

Whatever your circumstances always remember: If it is God who joins you together, you will never be alone.

Principle #9: Beware of being too "nice."

Let's say your older sister decides that it would be so charming for your favorite niece, her daughter, to be a flower girl in your wedding. Lovely thought. Just one problem: She will be exactly two-and-one-half years old. Either:

- She will steal the show from the bride; or
- She cannot reach the end of the aisle without halting halfway or wandering astray, thereby inciting giggles, promptings, and whispers; or
- All goes beautifully, as planned.

Take your chances. The risk is yours, but the risk is there.

Or consider the offers, usually from friends or relations wanting to be helpful, to play or sing, to take the photographs or fix the flowers. Inviting them to share in your day in any of these ways could add to its meaning and luster. Or you could be inviting disaster. Be careful to determine which result is more likely. Think of the person's qualifications, abilities, and time, and politely decline well-meaning offers from those whom you cannot truly rely on to do the job you expect. (Remember the story of the bride caught halfway down the aisle.)

Principle #10: In the end, every marriage is "perfect."

Countless marriage "fairs," directors, and guidebooks will tell you how to have the "perfect" wedding—often at the expense of many thousands of dollars. They will involve dressmakers and caterers, photographers and videographers, horse-and-carriage drivers, limousine services, florists, restaurateurs and country club managers, printers, hairdressers and manicurists and pedicurists, and salesfolk of every sort.

They're all wrong.

What makes a wedding "perfect" is when a couple join together in love and in the eyes of God, and all of that is right and good.

What doesn't matter so much is all the stuff which surrounds it. What doesn't matter is whether everything comes off perfectly.

Technically, as a production, there may be great room for improvement. But a wedding is not a show, no matter how much it may seem like one beforehand. Dramatic? Yes—a moment when we witness the activity of God in a deeply personal way. When family and friends gather together out of love and joy, the bride is always beautiful, the groom is always handsome, the service (so lovely anyway) is always graceful. And that is what matters.

I once flubbed my lines in a big way that was heard throughout the church, even caught on videotape for posterity. No matter. Bride and groom were united in Holy Matrimony; and, therefore, it was perfect. We need not worry about the gaffes or errors; let's avoid them if possible, but keep our focus on what truly does matter. God sees to the rest. And, as Genesis is wont to say, "It is very good."

For the technicalities and details and headaches of weddings all yield to a greater verity, one which sweeps up bride and groom, celebrant and congregation in a drama which lifts us to the heavens. An English priest used a different but vibrant image: "Marriage in Christian reality is...a roaring lion with strength and vigor and health and dignity that challenge faithful and faithless alike to reach out for a better way of living together under the shadow of the King of Kings and Lord of Lords."[67]

Holy Matrimony can bring alive the promises of God.

Notes

1. Quoted in Eric Josef Carlson, *Marriage and the English Reformation* (Oxford: Blackwell, 1994), 10.

2. A recent Rutgers sociological study, utilizing the work of a University of Chicago demographer, cited one of the benefits of marriage over cohabitation: "[t]he better connection of married couples to the larger community" of individuals and groups, such as in-laws, and social institutions, such as churches and synagogues. "These can be important sources of social and emotional support and material benefits." David Popenoe and Barbara Dafoe Whitehead, "Should We Live Together? What Young Adults Need to Know about Cohabitation before Marriage" (Brunswick, NJ: The National Marriage Project, January 1999), 12.

3. On both counts, note the canons (laws) of the Episcopal Church, e.g., Title I, Canon 18.1. The Episcopal Church, *Constitution & Canons* (1997). All canonical references hereafter are from the 1997 canons.

4. Marion J. Hatchett, *Commentary on the American Prayer Book* (New York: Seabury Press, 1980), 427.

5. *Oxford English Dictionary* (hereafter *OED*) (2nd ed., 1989), s.v. "ban" and "banns." The Anglo-Saxon word *gebann* is related to the Medieval Latin *bannum* [*Dictionary of Medieval Latin from British Sources* (London: Oxford University Press, 1975), I, 180].

6. Carlson, *Marriage and the English Reformation*, 24.

7. George S. Tyack, *Lore and Legend of the English Church* (London: William Andrews & Co., 1899), 179–180.

8. Canon I.18.

9. At least as recently as several decades ago, canons of the Church of England required a "table of kindred and affinity" to be posted in every parish church:

A man may not marry his	A woman may not marry with her
mother	father
daughter	son
adopted daughter	adopted son
father's mother	father's father
mother's mother	mother's father
son's daughter	son's son
daughter's daughter	daughter's son
sister	brother
wife's mother	husband's father
wife's daughter	husband's son
father's wife	mother's husband
son's wife	daughter's husband
father's father's wife	father's mother's husband
mother's father's wife	mother's mother's husband
wife's father's mother	husband's father's father
wife's mother's mother	husband's mother's father
wife's daughter's daughter	husband's son's son

A man may not marry his   A woman may not marry with her

wife's son's daughter	husband's daughter's son
son's son's wife	son's daughter's husband
daughter's son's wife	daughter's daughter's husband
father's sister	father's brother
mother's sister	mother's brother
brother's daughter	brother's son
sister's daughter	sister's son

In this Table the term "brother" includes half brothers and the term "sister" includes half sisters. [*The Canons of the Church of England* (London: SPCK, 1969), B 31 (p. 23).] Some, clearly, anticipate relationships after the death of one spouse. (But, one wonders, what would American "daytime dramas" do?)

10. Carlson, *Marriage and the English Reformation*, 25.

11. The necessity of free will is specified in the Episcopal Church's canon I.18.2(c).

12. See Canon I.18.2(b).

13. See Canon I.18.3(d–g).

14. Charlotte Brontë, *Jane Eyre* (London: Penguin Books, n.d.), 319 [ch. 26].

15. "When marital unity is imperiled by dissension, it shall be the duty of either or both parties, before contemplating legal action, to lay the matter before a Member of the Clergy; and it shall be the duty of such Member of the Clergy to labor that the parties may be reconciled." Canon I.19.1.

16. Oscar Wilde, *The Importance of Being Ernest*, Act III.

17. Canon I.18.2(b).

18. Canon I.18.3(a).

19. Canon I.18.3(e–g). The canon immediately following it (I.18.4) should also be carefully noted: "It shall be within the discretion of any Member of the Clergy of this Church to decline to solemnize any marriage."

20. Canon I.18.3(b). In addition to the required presence of the witnesses, the service notes "the presence of this company"; it includes the optional presentation of the bride (and groom if desired), and it invites the response of the people in the prayers, particularly in the intercessions which, as shall be seen (see sections "The Prayers" and "The Intercessions"), pay special notice of the couple's place within the wider society. See Kenneth W. Stevenson, *To Join Together: The Rite of Marriage* (New York: Pueblo Publishing Co., 1987), 154f.

21. In England, with its established religion, marriages are by law *only* allowed at the civic Registry Office, in a Church (i.e. Church of England), or in some other building set apart for religious purposes by a denomination or body.

22. Both "matrimony" and "marriage" entered the English language from Old French words which themselves derived from Latin; but the basic root of "marriage" in Latin is that for "husband" (*marīt-us*) whereas the Latin that gives us "matrimony" stems from the same as for "maternal," "mother" (*matr-em*). See *OED* s.v. "matrimony" and "marriage."

23. *OED*, s.v. "contract," "covenant." I am grateful to Prof. Andrew McThenia, who teaches contract law at Washington and Lee University, for the distinction.

24. Also 1 Corinthians 11:25; 2 Cor. 3:6; Hebrews 8:6–13, 9:15, 12:24.

25. *The Hymnal 1982* (New York: Church Hymnal Corp., 1982), #199; see also, less

familiarly, #187, "Through the Red Sea brought at last," and #202, "The Lamb's high banquet called to share."

26. Cf. *OED*, s.v. "adorn."

27. John Macquarrie, *A Guide to the Sacraments* (New York: Continuum, 1997), 215.

28. Some qualities of Jesus in his relationships with others:

accepting	full of expectation	self-giving
accountable/holding responsible	generous	self-sacrificing
altruistic	giving hope	sensitive
assertive (when needed!)	guiding	setting example
benevolent	healing	sorrowful/feeling deeply for
calling forth the best	holy	suffering
caring	honest	sympathetic
challenging	humble	teaching
cherishing	insightful	tender
compassionate	just	thankful
courteous	kind	thoughtful
determined	liberating	tolerant
didactic	loving	tough
disciplined	mentoring	trustful
educating/educing/ bringing forth	merciful	unconditional
embracing	mysterious	understanding
empathetic	nurturing	unlimited
fair	obedient	uplifting
faithful	passionate	vulnerable
fearless	patient	wise
forgiving	peaceful	with humor
forthright	realistic	with dignity
	respecting/respectful	

In asking this question, I have often noticed how much a couple reveal about themselves by the nature of the answers they give as to how they see and understand Jesus, appreciating the qualities our Lord shows forth.

29. John Booty, ed., *The Book of Common Prayer 1559: The Elizabethan Prayer Book* (Charlottesville, The University Pres of Virginia/Folger Shakespeare Library, 1976), 290f.

30. Macquarie, *Guide*, 219.

31. Research by the National Marriage Project suggests the "higher levels of productivity" attained by the married, versus cohabiters, arising from the ability to "specialize" in tasks over the long term. David Popenoe and Barbara Dafoe Whitehead, "The State of Our Unions: The Social Health of Marriage in America" (Brunswick, NJ: The National Marriage Project, June 1999), 4; and "Should We Live Together?," 12.

32. See BCP 1559, 291 n . 1; and *OED*, s.v. "comfort."

33. Popenoe and Whitehead, "Should We Live Together," 13.

34. See also Revelation 19:7–8.

35. Aimé-Georges Martimort, "The Contribution of Liturgical History to the Theology of Marriage," in Richard Malone and John R. Connery, eds., *Contemporary Perspectives on Christian Marriage* (Chicago: Loyola University Press, 1984), 310; BCP 1559, 290, 295; see also BCP 1549 and BCP 1552, e.g., as in *The First and Second Prayer Books of Edward VI* (London: J. M. Dent & Sons Ltd., n.d.), 252, 410.

36. BCP 1662, 302; 1928 BCP of the Episcopal Church, 300.

37. Stevenson, *To Join Together*, 8, 50. Stevenson is an Anglican writing on the Roman Catholic rite.

38. Hatchett, *Commentary*, 435.

39. E.g., Hebrews 4:14.

40. This movement at this particular point is a custom of relatively recent origin, not expected in this or any previous Prayer Book, though in England the couple would kneel "afore the Lord's Table" for the Lord's Prayer and other petitions [BCP 1552]. See *Prayer Book Studies*, No. X (New York: The Church Pension Fund, 1958), 6; and Byron D. Stuhlman, *Prayer Book Rubrics Expanded* (New York: Church Hymnal Corp., 1987), 155f., who indicates, following English custom, that approaching the altar prior to the blessing is admissible.

41. See Popenoe and Whitehead, "Should We Live Together," which reviews social science evidence suggesting "that living together is not a good way to prepare for marriage or to avoid divorce. What's more, it shows that the rise in cohabitation is not a positive family trend. Cohabiting unions tend to weaken the institution of marriage and pose clear and present dangers for women and children." For example, "the research indicates that:

"Living together before marriage increases the risk of breaking up after marriage.

"Living together outside of marriage increases the risk of domestic violence for women, and the risk of physical and sexual abuse for children.

"Unmarried couples have lower levels of happiness and well-being than married couples." (p. 4).

42. Edmund S. Morgan, *The Puritan Dilemma*, ed. Oscar Handlin (Boston: Little, Brown & Co., 1958), 53.

43. C. S. Lewis, quoted in Helge Rubinstein, *The Oxford Book of Marriage* (Oxford & New York: Oxford University Press, 1990), 130.

44. BCP, 486 (Burial Office), alluding to Revelation 14:13.

45. Martimort, "The Contribution of Liturgical History," 300.

46. George Harford & Morley Stevenson, eds., *Prayer Book Dictionary* (New York: Longmans, Green, & Co., 1912), 623, though Tyack omits the placement of ring on thumb (*Lore and Legend*, 192f).

47. Tyack, *Lore and Legend*, 195f.

48. Horton Davies, *Worship and Theology in England: From Cranmer to Hooker 1534–1603* (Princeton, NJ: Princeton University Press, 1970), 262. The other two were making the sign of the cross on a child in baptism, and kneeling at Holy Communion.

49. Richard Hooker, *Of the Laws of Ecclesiastical Polity*, Book V, LXXII [6] (London: Dent, n.d.), II, 394.

50. BCP 1559, 292. English Prayer Books through 1662 also had the groom lay on the book the "accustomed duty" for the priest.

51. BCP 1552, 1662. The 1549 added, as the second clause, "this gold and silver I thee give." See Hatchett, *Commentary*, 436.

52. BCP 1928, 302.

53. "[T]he fact that a marriage has to be 'consummated' by the sexual act, otherwise the marriage is considered null, as if it had never taken place at all, is a clear indication that the sexual relation is indeed part of the matter of the sacrament, and in some cultures the ceremonies are not complete until the newly-wed couple have been installed in the house where they will cohabit as man and wife." Macquarrie, *Guide*, 220.

54. Martimort, in Malone, 308, who says that the services of a priest were not considered essential for a valid marriage as late as the ninth century in the Eastern church, and in the West until the sixteenth century (though note that the 1549 BCP presumes one). On the issue of ministers of this sacrament, see Macquarrie, *Guide*, 220, and the entire chapter on Marriage for a broader understanding of how this is manifested in the couple and their actions, including sexual intercourse, and how the priest serves to represent the Church at large.

55. The practice emerged from Post-Tridentine Roman Catholicism; see Stevenson, 115f, who reckons that Thomas "Cranmer would have turned in his grave...since the priestly symbolism eloquently denies completely the nonpriestly and nonsacramental intention of the original liturgical reformers," of whom Cranmer was a leader. Stuhlman agrees on the point (*Prayer Book Rubrics Expanded*, 156).

56. See Matthew 19:4–6, which is based on Genesis 2:24.

57. See esp. Romans 8:29 ("For those whom he foreknew he also predestined to be conformed to the image of his Son"); Romans 12:2 ("Do not be conformed to this world, but be transformed by the renewing of your minds"); and Philippians 3:21 ("He will transform the body of our humiliation that it may be conformed to the body of his glory, by the power that also enables him to make all things subject to himself.").

58. Erich Segal, *Love Story* (New York: Harper & Row, 1970), 131.

59. Deborah Tannen, "I'm Sorry, I Won't Apologize," *The New York Times Magazine* (July 21, 1996), 34. "The other day my husband said to me, 'I'm sorry I hurt your feelings.' I knew he was really trying. He has learned, through our years together, that apologies are important to me. But he was grinning, because he also knew that 'I'm sorry I hurt your feelings' left open the possibility—indeed, strongly suggested— that he regretted not what he did but my emotional reaction."

60. See Stevenson, *To Join Together*, 50 and passim.

61. A "signet ring" which bore a person's seal was commonly used to ratify documents ("signed and sealed") by embedding the ring in sealing wax; a vestige of this is found in the Episcopal Church by bishops who use their episcopal rings, engraved with their seal, to attest to ordinations of clergy. Hatchett, *Commentary*, 437, suggests that the veil is a remnant of the Orthodox crowns. In one of the more publicized of Anglican weddings, the Archbishop of Canterbury Robert Runcie (himself a scholar of the Orthodox tradition) referred to this practice at the nuptials of Prince Charles and Lady Diana Spencer, observing that through this custom is expressed "the conviction that as husband and wife they are Kings and Queens of Creation" (*The [London] Times*, July 30, 1981, 3).

62. Stevenson, *To Join Together*, 30ff, 93. For Roman Catholics, "Matrimony is normally to be celebrated in the mass," i.e. Eucharist, according to the Second Vatican Council

(Constitution on the Sacred Liturgy, Chapter II, sec. 77 [quoted in ibid., 125]). The 1549, 1552, and 1559 BCPs all conclude the order for matrimony with the instruction, "The newe maried persones (the same daye of their mariage) must receiue the holy communion." By 1662, though, the commandment had become mere encouragement, which itself was dropped in American Prayer Books. By 1958 the Standing Liturgical Commission was again commending it as "a fitting climax of the nuptial rites" (*Prayer Book Studies*, 8).

63. 1 Chronicles 29:14 (1928 BCP, 73).

64. BCP, 423 (at the entrance), 425 (after the consents), 426 (following lessons), 431(at the exit), or at the Offertory. It is vital to match hymns with congregation—that is, for the congregation to be large enough to sustain a hymn, and for the hymn to be one which the congregation is able to sing. The parish clergy and musician can be extremely helpful.

65. See also Matthew 9:15; Mark 2:19–20; Luke 5:34–35; and John 3:29.

66. Stevenson, for example, argues for restoring the holding of crowns above the couple during the blessing (from the Eastern Orthodox tradition); holding a canopy above them during the prayers (as Swedish Lutherans do); anointing them (as in the Coptic rite); or even binding them together with a lasso (as in one Hispanic custom). *To Join Together*, 196ff.

67. Ibid., 234.